KS1 MATHS
SATs SUCCESS
PRACTICE TEST PAPERS

KS1
MATHS
SATs

complete tests

PRACTICE
TEST
PAPERS

ALAN DOBBS

Contents

(pull-out section at the back of the book)

Introduction and instructions

How these tests will help your child

This book is made up of three complete sets of practice test papers. Each set contains similar test papers to those that your child will take in maths at the end of Year 2. The tests will assess your child's knowledge, skills and understanding in the areas of study undertaken since they began Year 1. These practice test papers can be used any time throughout the year to provide practice for the Key Stage 1 tests.

The results of each set of papers will provide a good idea of the strengths and weaknesses of your child.

Administering the tests

* Provide your child with a quiet environment where they can complete each test undisturbed.
* Provide your child with a pen or pencil and an eraser. A ruler is allowed for Paper 2 but a calculator is **not** allowed in either paper.
* The amount of time given for each test varies, so remind your child at the start of each one how long they have and give them access to a clock or watch.
  You should only read the instructions out to your child, not the actual questions (except the aural questions).
* Although handwriting is not assessed, remind your child that their answers should be clear.
  Advise your child that if they are unable to do one of the questions, they should go on to the next one and come back to it later, if they have time. If they finish before the end, they should go back and check their work.

Paper 1: arithmetic

* All answers are worth 1 mark, with a total number of 25 marks for each test.
* Your child will have approximately **20 minutes** to complete the test.
* The questions test your child's understanding and application of number, calculations and fractions.
* Both formal and informal methods of answering mathematical problems are acceptable.

Paper 2: reasoning

* All answers are worth 1 mark (unless stated), with a total number of 35 marks for each test.
* Your child will have approximately **35 minutes** to complete the test, including 5 minutes for the aural questions.
* The first five questions should be read out to your child. Using the aural questions administration guide on pages 95–96, read each question and remember to repeat the bold text.
* Questions will test calculation, data gathering and interpretation, shape, space and measures. They will test your child's ability to use maths in contextualised, abstract and real-life situations.

Marking the practice test papers

The answers have been provided to enable you to check how your child has performed. Fill in the marks that your child achieved for each part of the tests.

Please note: these tests are **only a guide** to the mark your child can achieve and cannot guarantee the same is achieved during the Key Stage 1 tests, as the mark needed to achieve the expected standard varies from year to year.

	Set A	Set B	Set C
Paper 1: arithmetic	/25	/25	/25
Paper 2: reasoning	/35	/35	/35
Total	/60	/60	/60

The scores achieved on these practice test papers will help to show if your child is working at the expected standard in maths:

20–30 = working towards the expected standard
31–42 = working at the expected standard
43–60 = working above the expected standard.

When an area of weakness has been identified, it is useful to go over these, and similar types of questions, with your child. Sometimes your child will be familiar with the subject matter but might not understand what the question is asking. This will become apparent when talking to your child.

Shared marking and target setting

Engaging your child in the marking process will help them to develop a greater understanding of the tests and, more importantly, provide them with some ownership of their learning. They will be able to see more clearly how and why certain areas have been identified for them to target for improvement.

Top tips for your child

Don't make silly mistakes. Make sure you emphasise to your child the importance of reading the question. Easy marks can be picked up by just doing as the question asks.

Make answers clearly legible. If your child has made a mistake, encourage them to put a cross through it and write the correct answer clearly next to it. Try to encourage your child to use an eraser as little as possible.

Don't panic! These practice test papers, and indeed the end of Key Stage 1 tests, are meant to provide a guide to the standard a child has attained. They are not the be-all and end-all, as children are assessed regularly throughout the school year. Explain to your child that there is no need to worry if they cannot do a question – tell them to go on to the next question and come back to the problematic question later if they have time.

Key Stage 1

Maths

Paper 1: arithmetic

Time:

You have approximately **20 minutes** to complete this test paper.

Maximum mark	Actual mark
25	

First name	
Last name	

Practice question

$$5 - 1 = \boxed{}$$

1

$5 + 3 =$ ☐

2

$10 - 3 =$ ☐

3

$10 \div 2 =$ ☐

4 $12 + \boxed{} = 19$

○

5 $10 + 11 = \boxed{}$

○

6 $\frac{1}{4}$ of $20 = \boxed{}$

○

7

$5 \times 2 = 12 -$ ⬚

8

⬚ $- 16 = 16$

9

$5 \times 3 =$ ⬚

10

$\frac{3}{4}$ of 20 = [   ]

○

11

99 = 59 + [   ]

○

12

$47 = 25 +$ ⬚

13

$80 \div 10 =$ ⬚

14

$$\boxed{} - 14 = 30$$

15

$$25 + 16 = 41$$

$$41 - \boxed{} = 16$$

16

$$15 + 6 + 8 = \boxed{}$$

17

$$\frac{1}{2} \text{ of } \boxed{} = 20$$

18

$$20 \div 2 = 2 \times \boxed{}$$

19

$$18 = \frac{1}{2} \text{ of } \boxed{}$$

20

$$30 \div \boxed{} = 2 \times 5$$

21

$$20 \times 2 = \boxed{}$$

22

$\dfrac{1}{3}$ of 21 = ⬚

○

23

45 + 13 + 2 = ⬚

○

24

$\dfrac{2}{4}$ of 10 = ⬜

25

12 = $\dfrac{1}{2}$ of ⬜

Key Stage 1

Maths

Paper 2: reasoning

You will need to ask someone to read the instructions to you for the first five questions. These can be found on page 95. You can answer the remaining questions on your own.

Time:

You have approximately **35 minutes** to complete this test paper. This timing includes approximately 5 minutes for the aural questions.

Maximum mark	Actual mark
35	

First name	
Last name	

Practice question

1

2

	stickers

00 g   3 kg   20 kg   100 kg

P

Now continue with the rest of the paper on your own.

6 Look at these signs.

| + | = | − |

Write a sign in each box to make this correct.

23 ⬚ 8 ⬚ 15

7 This sentence is correct.

15 is more than **10** ✓

Four of these sentences are correct.

Tick (✓) them.

45 is less than **57** ☐

34 is more than **27** ☐

69 is more than **96** ☐

81 is equal to **18** ☐

28 is less than **34** ☐

59 is more than **7** ☐

There are **26** children.

8 children are drawing.

How many children are **not drawing**?

┌─────────────────────────────┐
│   │
│   children   │
└─────────────────────────────┘   ◯

9 Some of these numbers are **even**.

Circle the **even** numbers.

13   16   29   33   76   50   27   ◯

10 Complete this table.

The first row has been done for you.

	2×5	10
		20

11 Put these numbers in order from **least** to **most**.

14   98   37   78   100   29   16

least   most

12 Circle $\frac{3}{4}$ of the bananas.

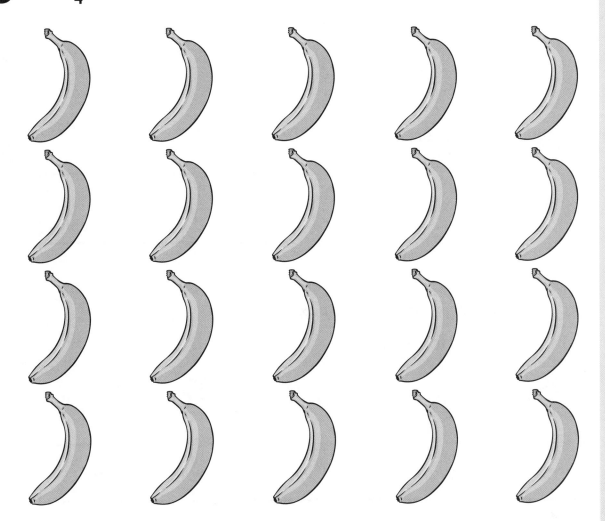

13 Shade this jug to show 650 ml.

14

How many 10p coins are there in £1.50?

10p coins

15 Write each number in the correct box.

One has been done for you.

51   28   16   43   32   34

Numbers less than 30	Numbers more than 30
16	

16 Look at these cards.

Use each card once to write each of these number sentences.

17 Tick (✓) the two shapes that are hexagons.

18 Pineapples cost 50p each. Oranges cost 10p each.

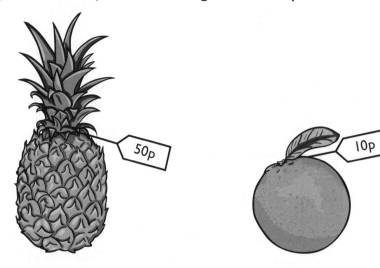

Adam buys **2** pineapples and **3** oranges.

How much change does he get from £1.50?

Show your working	

p

2 mark

19 There are **100** pieces in a kit.

15 pieces have been lost.

How many pieces remain?

pieces

20 Class 5 have made a bar chart.

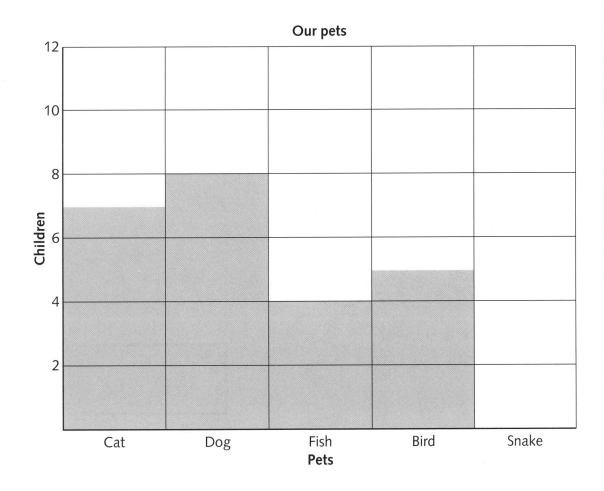

a) 3 children have a snake.

Show this on the bar chart. ◯

b) More children have a cat than a fish.

How many more?

	children

◯

21 Complete the sequences.

a)

◯

b)

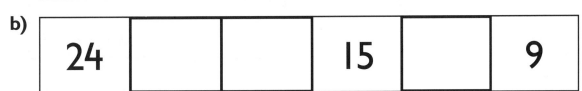

◯

22 Look at the thermometer.

25 °C
20 °C
15 °C
10 °C
5 °C
0 °C

What temperature is shown?

°C

○

23

| I whole | $\frac{1}{4}$ | $\frac{3}{4}$ | $\frac{1}{2}$ |

a) Join the fractions to the correct pizza.

b) Add the total amount of pizza.

How many **whole** pizzas?

whole pizzas ○

24 Draw the hands on the analogue (dial) clocks so that they show the following times.

half past 8

quarter past 6

5 o'clock

25 Estimate the number marked by the arrow.

Write the number in the box.

26 Look at this arrow.

You turn the arrow one clockwise quarter turn.

Tick (✓) the arrow that shows how it looks after the turn.

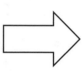

27 Match the correct name with each 3-D shape.

Cube

Cylinder

Pyramid

Cuboid

28 This reel has 1 m of tape.

Hamid needs to cut the tape into 20 cm pieces.

How many pieces will he have if he uses all of the tape?

pieces

○

29

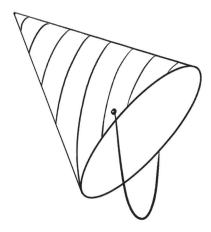

Party hats are sold in packs of 5.

Jane needs 27 hats for her party.

How many packs of hats should she buy?

packs

○

30 Mark the vertices that you can see on this cube by circling them.

31 Circle the bee that is 6th from the left.

Key Stage 1

Maths

Maths

Paper 1: arithmetic

PAPER 1

Time:

You have approximately **20 minutes** to complete this test paper.

Maximum mark	Actual mark
25	....

First name	
Last name	

Practice question

$5 + 7 =$ ☐

1

$99 + 1 =$ ☐

2

$30 \div 2 =$ ☐

3

$11 + 3 + 5 =$ ☐

4

$$\boxed{} = \frac{1}{4} \text{ of } 40$$

5

$$44 - \boxed{} = 30$$

6

$$\frac{3}{4} \text{ of } 12 = \boxed{}$$

7

$40 + \boxed{} = 100$

$100 = 60 + \boxed{}$

8

$14 - \boxed{} = 7$

9

$10 \times 10 = \boxed{}$

10

$\frac{1}{3}$ of 30 =

11

56 – 31 =

12

$15 + 7 + 9 = \boxed{}$

○

13

$15 + \boxed{} = 35$

○

14

Half of 20 = ⬚

15

$25 \div 5 =$ ⬚

2018 Letts Educational, an imprint of HarperCollinsPublishers Ltd – not to be photocopied.

39

16

$5 \times 0 =$ ☐

17

☐ $+ 34 = 64$

18

$25 - 6 - 2 =$ [ ]

19

$\dfrac{3}{4}$ of $100 =$ [ ]

20

$$5 + 5 + 20 = \boxed{}$$

○

21

$$67 - \boxed{} = 25$$

○

22

$$25 + \boxed{} = 50$$

○

23

$$100 - \boxed{} = 60$$

○

24

$\dfrac{1}{3}$ of 66 =

25

50 × ☐ = 100

Key Stage 1

Maths

Paper 2: reasoning

You will need to ask someone to read the instructions to you for the first five questions. These can be found on page 96. You can answer the remaining questions on your own.

Time:

You have approximately **35 minutes** to complete this test paper. This timing includes approximately 5 minutes for the aural questions.

Maximum mark	Actual mark
35	

First name	
Last name	

Practice question

stickers

1

2

3

┌─────────────────────────┐
│   │
│   │
└─────────────────────────┘

4

┌─────────────────────────────────┐
│   faces │
└─────────────────────────────────┘

5

0 minutes   **30 minutes**   **2 hours**   **12 hours**

┌──┐
│   Now continue with the rest of the paper on your own. │
└──┘

6 Tara is standing next to her sunflower. Tara is 1 metre tall.

Tick (✓) the height that you estimate the sunflower to be.

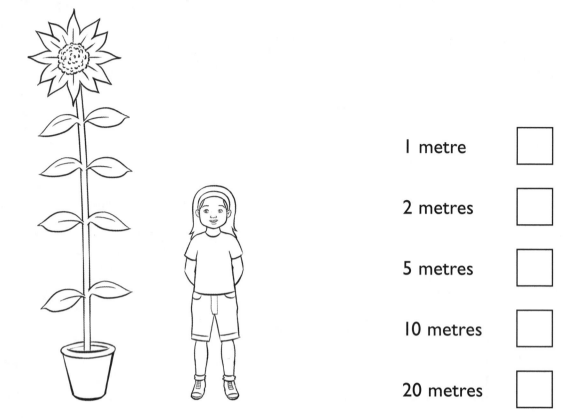

1 metre ☐

2 metres ☐

5 metres ☐

10 metres ☐

20 metres ☐

7 Look at the grid.

One of the squares is shaded.

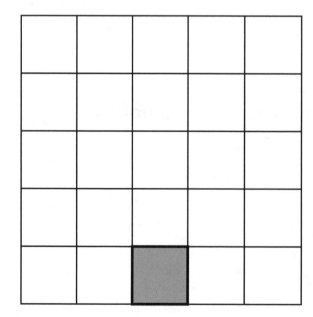

Start at the shaded square.

Move 3 squares up and 2 squares left.

Shade the square that you are now on.

8 Write the missing number.

An example has been done for you.

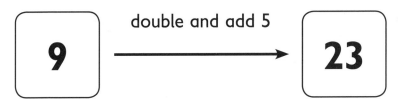

| 9 | double and add 5 → | 23 |

| 7 | double and add 5 → | ☐ |

○

9

Yasmin has emptied her money box.

She needs 56p for a set of pens.

Write 2 different ways that Yasmin could pay for the pens using her coins.

1	2

○

2 marks

10 Write a number that is between these numbers.

| 80 | ← | | → | 100 |

11 There are 50 balloons in a box.

17 balloons are green.

20 balloons are blue.

The rest of the balloons are yellow.

How many balloons are yellow?

Show your working

_____ balloons

2 mark

12 Sort the numbers into this Venn diagram. Some of the numbers cannot be used.

35 16 40 15 27 36 53

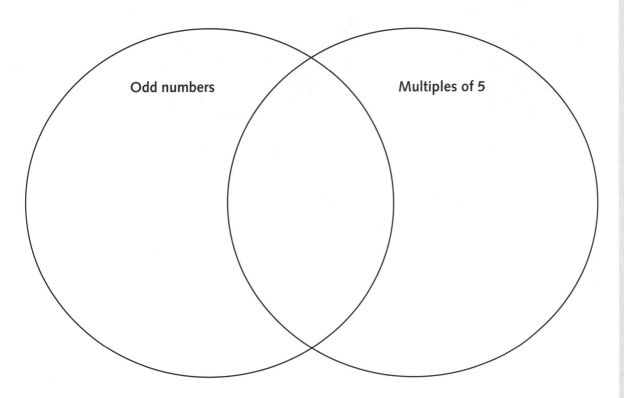

Odd numbers

Multiples of 5

13 Look at this number sequence.

1st	2nd	3rd	4th
18	21	24	27

What would the next number in this sequence be?

2018 Letts Educational, an imprint of HarperCollinsPublishers Ltd – not to be photocopied.

51

14 Ali went to the market to buy fruit.

Apples 15p

Bananas 25p

He wants to buy 2 bananas and 1 apple.

How much money will Ali need?

P

15 **Two** of these sentences describe true properties of a cylinder.

Tick (✓) the correct sentences.

Cylinders have 2 circular faces.

Cylinders have more than 4 corners.

Cylinders do not have right-angle vertices.

Cylinders have 3 triangular faces.

16 Fran made a tally of the birds visiting her garden.

Bird	Tally	Total
Robin	||||	
Finch	�334 �334 |	
Pigeon	�334	
Starling	�334 �334 ||	
Thrush	�334 |||	

Help Fran by adding the totals to her chart.

17 Look at this grid.

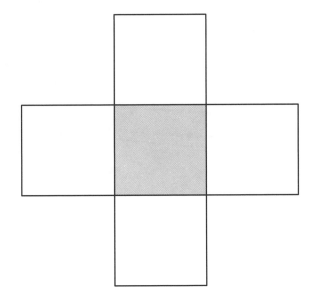

Put an X in the square above the shaded square.

Put a Y in the square below the shaded square.

2018 Letts Educational, an imprint of HarperCollinsPublishers Ltd – not to be photocopied.

53

18 Write an equivalent fraction.

One has been done for you.

$\frac{4}{4}$ = | I whole |

$\frac{3}{3}$ =

$\frac{2}{4}$ =

$\frac{3}{2}$ =

19 Eric wants to fill his fish tank.

The fish tank holds 22 litres of water.

The jug holds 2 litres of water.

How many full jugs of water will Eric need?

jugs

20 Is each statement always, sometimes or never true?

Write **always**, **sometimes** or **never** in each box.

always	sometimes	never

Multiples of 3 end in 1.		

Multiples of 5 end in 2.		

Multiples of 10 end in 0.		

21 Draw the reflection of this shape using the dotted mirror line.

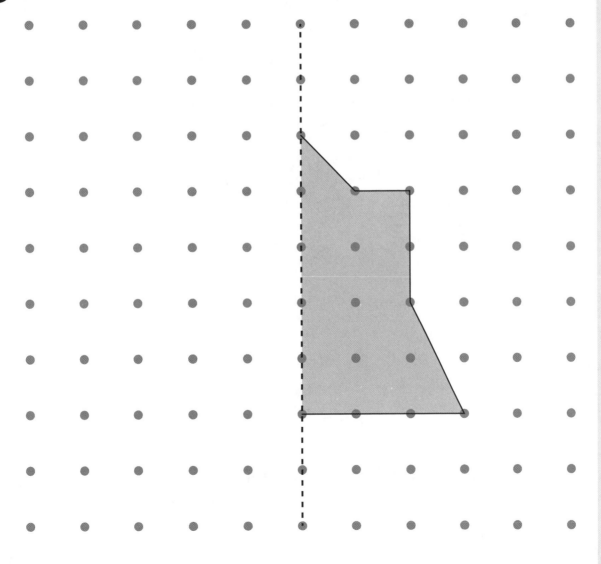

22 Add 10 to each of these numbers.

One has been done for you.

87 ⟶ | 97 |

23 ⟶ | |

47 ⟶ | |

64 ⟶ | |

23 Martina wants to make some biscuits.

For her biscuits Martina needs:

150 g flour

100 g butter

50 g dried fruit

50 g sugar

What is the total weight of Martina's ingredients?

| g |

24 Gabby walks to school.

She leaves home at half past seven.

Her journey takes 45 minutes.

a) Draw hands on the analogue (dial) clock to show the time that Gabby leaves home.

b) Draw hands on the analogue (dial) clock to show the time that Gabby arrives at school.

25 Liz's cat Smudge eats 2 packets of food each day.

How many packets of food does Smudge eat in 1 week?

Show your working

packets

2 mar

26 Shema has found that 2 crayons are the same length as the top of her book.

Estimate the number of crayons that Shema would need to go around the whole book.

crayons

27 Frankie buys a burger.

He pays with a £2 coin.

Frankie gets 50p change.

How much did the burger cost?

£ _____

○

28 Draw the next three shapes in this sequence.

    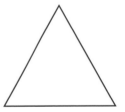

_____   _____   _____

○

29 Use a ruler to draw a line that is 10 cm in length.

30 Write the answers in the boxes.

81 $\xrightarrow{\text{take away 10}}$ [ ]

46 $\xrightarrow{\text{take away 10}}$ [ ]

97 $\xrightarrow{\text{take away 10}}$ [ ]

Key Stage 1

Maths

Paper 1: arithmetic

Time:

You have approximately **20 minutes** to complete this test paper.

Maximum mark	Actual mark
25	

First name	
Last name	

Practice question

$2 \times 3 =$ ☐

1

$6 \div 2 = \boxed{}$

2

$\boxed{} = \dfrac{1}{2}$ of 24

3

$20 - 14 = \boxed{}$

4

$\boxed{} + 12 = 38$

5

$5 \times \boxed{} = 30$

6

$12 \div 2 = \boxed{}$

7

$67 - 15 = \boxed{}$

8

$97 - 55 = \boxed{}$

9

$\boxed{} - 9 = 19$

10 $\boxed{} \times 10 = 70$

11 $\boxed{} + 89 = 99$

12

$$\boxed{} - 12 = 43$$

$$43 + 12 = \boxed{}$$

13

$$\frac{1}{4} \text{ of } 20 = \boxed{}$$

14

$24 \div \boxed{} = 12$

$\boxed{} \times 2 = 24$

15

$5 \times 3 = 3 + \boxed{}$

16

$\boxed{} \div 5 = 5$

17

$36 + \boxed{} = 60$

18

$\frac{1}{3}$ of 18 = [ ]

19

33 + 28 = [ ]

2018 Letts Educational, an imprint of HarperCollinsPublishers Ltd – not to be photocopied.

69

20

$47 - 22 = $

21

$\dfrac{1}{3}$ of $90 = $

22

$$20 \div \boxed{} = 4$$

$$\boxed{} \times 4 = 20$$

23

$$73 - 42 = \boxed{}$$

2018 Letts Educational, an imprint of HarperCollinsPublishers Ltd – not to be photocopied.

71

24

$\dfrac{1}{3}$ of 99 =

25

20 × [ ] = 100

Key Stage 1

Maths

Paper 2: reasoning

You will need to ask someone to read the instructions to you for the first five questions. These can be found on page 96. You can answer the remaining questions on your own.

Time:

You have approximately **35 minutes** to complete this test paper. This timing includes approximately 5 minutes for the aural questions.

Maximum mark	Actual mark
35	

First name	
Last name	

2018 Letts Educational, an imprint of HarperCollinsPublishers Ltd – not to be photocopied.

73

Practice question

| 3 | 6 | 9 | 12 | |

1

| | P | | | P | | | P |

○

2

○

3

| children |

4

| vertices |

5

itres   grams   centimetres   kilograms

Now continue with the rest of the paper on your own.

6 Write the same number in each box to make this correct.

$$\boxed{} \; + \; \boxed{} \; = \; 30$$

7 There are 10 satsumas in each bag and 8 more loose satsumas.

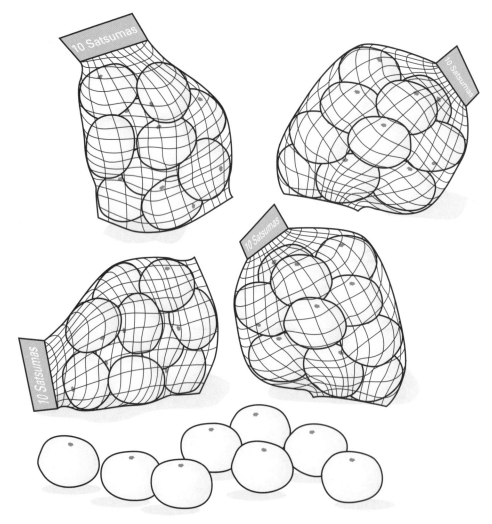

How many satsumas are there in total?

$$\boxed{}$$ satsumas

8 The two joined numbers add up to 18.

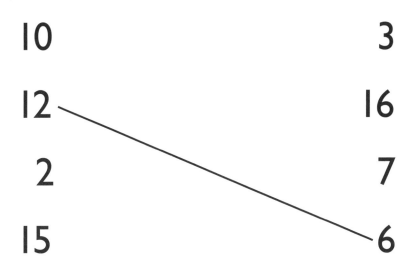

10   3

12   16

2   7

15   6

Join other numbers that have a total of 18.

◯

9 Henry has weighed this bowl.

He has 5 bowls to take to his friends, so they can all have a share of ice cream.

How much do Henry's bowls weigh in total?

g

◯

10 Ben worked out the correct answer to 50 ÷ 5.

His answer was 10.

Show how Ben could have worked this out.

11 Fill in the missing numbers.

a)

15		21		27

b)

55		45		35

12 This shape has been divided into equal parts.

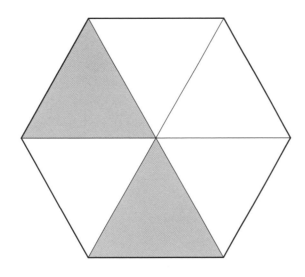

What fraction of the shape is shaded?

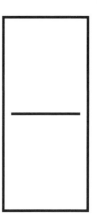

⃝

13 Circle the highest temperature.

20°C   22°C   18°C   21°C   12°C   ⃝

14 Nina and her class have made a chart.

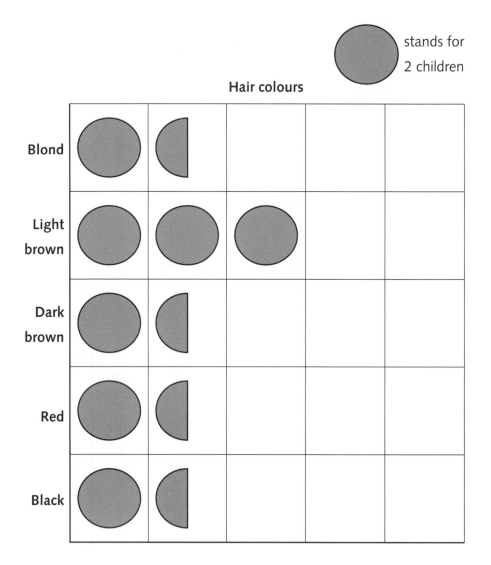

a) How many children have red hair?

	children

b) Only one hair colour shows an **even** number of children.

Which colour is it?

15 Circle the coldest temperature.

1°C   3°C   5°C   0°C   10°C

16 Look at the number machine.

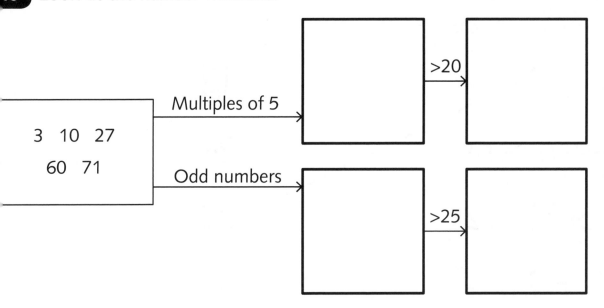

Put each number in the correct box(es).

○ 2 marks

17 Tara has made a list of chores.

Chores

8:00 am – Tidy bedroom

9:30 am – Walk the dog

10:15 am – Homework

12:00 noon – Wrap present

How long has Tara allowed to walk her dog?

minutes

○

2018 Letts Educational, an imprint of HarperCollinsPublishers Ltd – not to be photocopied.

81

18 Draw the missing lines.

One has been done for you.

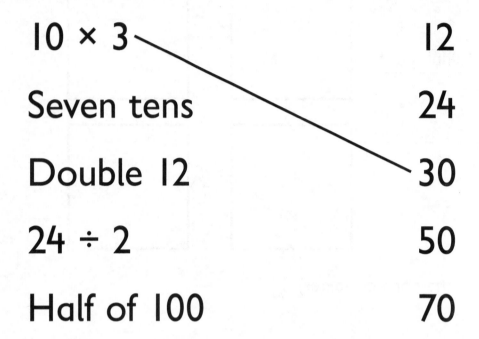

10 × 3   12

Seven tens   24

Double 12   30

24 ÷ 2   50

Half of 100   70

19 Alan is thinking of a number.

If he doubles his number and adds 7, the answer is 37.

Write the number that Alan is thinking of.

20 Shade the flash that is fourth from the right.

21 Hammed has found some card shapes.
He wants to make a cuboid.

Tick (✓) the 6 shapes that he should use.

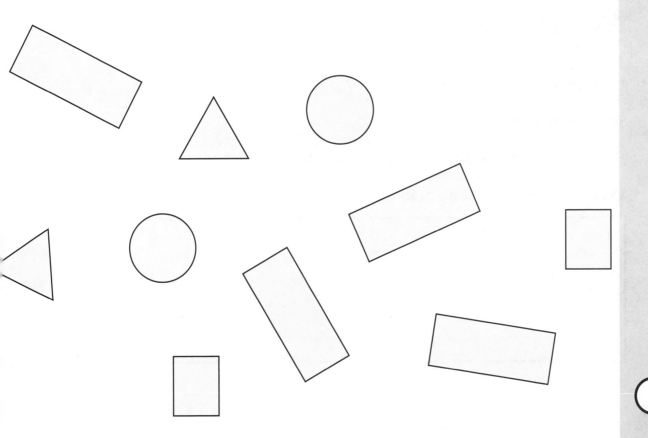

Alexi has emptied her money box.

She needs **87p**.

Alexi takes the amount needed using the coins from her box.

Write which coins she could choose to find the exact amount needed.

23 What is the capacity of the bottle most likely to be?

Circle the correct amount.

5 litres   **5 ml**   **2 litres**   **10 litres**   **50 ml**

Look at the grid.

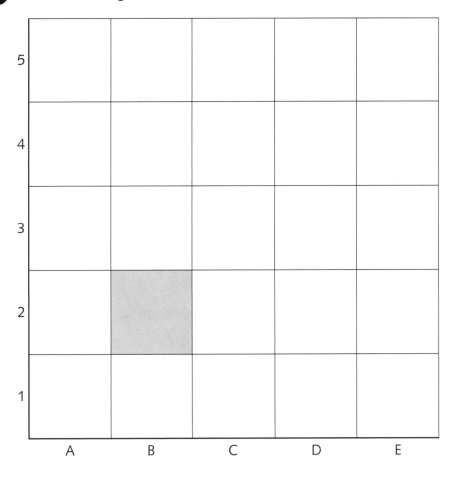

Square **B2** has been shaded.

Shade squares **C4**, **E3** and **D1**.

Jenny wants to buy a tablet computer that costs £90.

She saves £10 each week.

For how many weeks will she need to save until she has the right amount of money to buy the tablet computer?

weeks

26 Write the missing numbers.

a) $8 \times 10 = 94 - $ ☐

b) $50 \div 5 = 2 \times $ ☐

27 A group of children share 12 tomatoes.

Each child got 3 tomatoes.

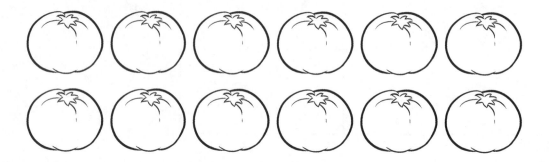

How many children shared the tomatoes?

☐ children

28 Shade more squares so that $\frac{3}{4}$ of the whole is shaded.

29 Write the numbers in the correct positions.

410   497   458

2018 Letts Educational, an imprint of HarperCollinsPublishers Ltd – not to be photocopied.

87

30 Class 2 have made a tally of the weather during March.

Weather in March

Weather	Tally	Total
Sunny	|||||	
Showers	||||| |||	
Cloudy	||||| |||||	
Rain	|||||	
Snow	|||	

a) Count the tallies and write the totals in the correct column.

b) Add the missing data from the tally to the block graph.

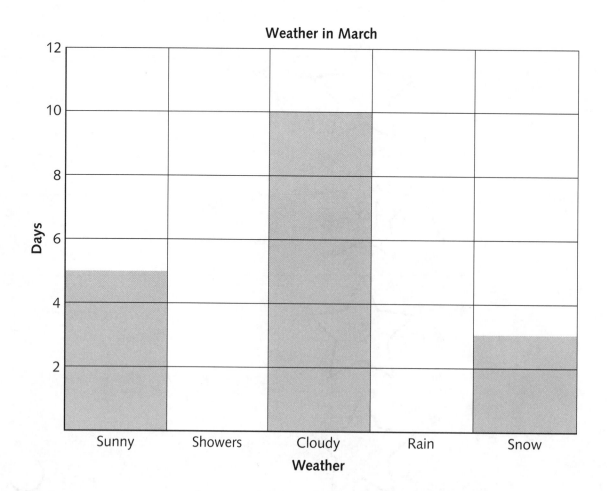

Weather in March

Answers and mark scheme

Notes to parents

Paper 1

These questions test calculating skills. An ability to work mentally will give a time advantage. Your child should be able to work with number facts to 20. (Children should know that 15 + 5 equals 20 and that 20 − 15 = 5; that 5 × 4 = 20 and that 20 ÷ 4 = 5.) Children should use this knowledge to extend their understanding of number facts to 100. Where the answer appears before the main content of the calculation, this tests your child's ability to use inverse (opposite) relationships between addition and subtraction. Knowing a fraction of a given quantity is an extension of your child's multiplication and division skills.

Paper 2

These questions test your child's ability to apply mathematics to problems and to reason, choosing an appropriate method to answer the question. The aural section will allow your child to become accustomed to the type of questions that they should expect and will experience during the actual tests at school.

The written questions test a wide variety of skills and the ability to choose a suitable mathematical strategy to answer the problems. Some of the questions provide an extra mark for showing how the problem was solved. This is an opportunity to see how your child is using the skills that are required to become a successful mathematician. Some of the questions require a range of skills, others are more straightforward.

Set A Paper 1

Practice question   4

1.	8	(1 mark)
2.	7	(1 mark)
3.	5	(1 mark)
4.	7	(1 mark)
5.	21	(1 mark)
6.	5	(1 mark)

7.	2	(1 mark)
8.	32	(1 mark)
9.	15	(1 mark)
10.	15	(1 mark)
11.	40	(1 mark)
12.	22	(1 mark)
13.	8	(1 mark)
14.	44	(1 mark)
15.	25	(1 mark)
16.	29	(1 mark)
17.	40	(1 mark)
18.	5	(1 mark)
19.	36	(1 mark)
20.	3	(1 mark)
21.	40	(1 mark)
22.	7	(1 mark)
23.	60	(1 mark)
24.	5	(1 mark)
25.	24	(1 mark)

Set A Paper 2

Practice question   A group of 6 caterpillars circled.

1.	19	(1 mark)
2.	25 stickers	(1 mark)
3.	(3 kg)	(1 mark)
4.	45p	(1 mark)
5.		(1 mark)

6. 23 $-$ 8 $=$ 15

   or 23 $=$ 8 $+$ 15   (1 mark)

7. 45 is less than 57 ✓
   34 is more than 27 ✓
   28 is less than 34 ✓
   59 is more than 7 ✓   (1 mark)

8. 18 children   (1 mark)

9. (16) (76) (50)　　　　　　　　**(1 mark)**

10.

2 × 5	10
4 × 5	20
6 × 5	30

　　　　　　　　　　　　(1 mark)

11.

14	16	29	37	78	98	100

least　　　　　　　　　　most

　　　　　　　　　　　　(1 mark)

12. 15 bananas circled.

This could be 3 lots of 5, 15 as a group or any 15 bananas in any combination. **(1 mark)**

13.

　　　　　　　　　　　　(1 mark)

14. 15 10p coins　　　　　**(1 mark)**

15.

Numbers less than 30	Numbers more than 30
16　28	51　43　32　34

　　　　　　　　　　　　(1 mark)

16. *Either 1 of the following multiplications and either 1 of the following divisions:*

2 × 4 = 8　　4 × 2 = 8

8 ÷ 4 = 2　　8 ÷ 2 = 4　　**(1 mark)**

17.

　　　　　　　　　　　　(1 mark)

18. 20p

Any method that shows the amount:

2 × 50p = £1　　　3 × 10p = 30p

£1 + 30p = £1.30

or

50p + 50p + 10p + 10p + 10p = £1.30

£1.50 − £1.30 = 20p

(2 marks for correct answer. Award 1 mark for using appropriate method but wrong answer given.)

19. 85 pieces　　　　　　　**(1 mark)**

20. a) Snake column shows 3.

Note: It is important that the graph shows an understanding of each square representing 2 items and that the 3 snakes are shown as a solid lower block of 2 and a split upper block counting as 1.

　　　　　　　　　　　　(1 mark)

b) 3 children　　　　　　**(1 mark)**

21. a)

2	5	8	11	14	17

　　　　　　　　　　　　(1 mark)

b)

24	21	18	15	12	9

　　　　　　　　　　　　(1 mark)

22. 16°C　　　　　　　　**(1 mark)**

23. a)

　　　　　　　　　　　　(1 mark)

b) 2 whole pizzas　　　**(1 mark)**

24.

　　　　　　　　　　　　(1 mark)

25. *Any number between* **65** *and* **75** *is acceptable.* **(1 mark)**

26.

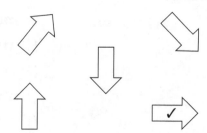

　　　　　　　　　　　　(1 mark)

27. Cube · Cylinder · Pyramid · Cuboid

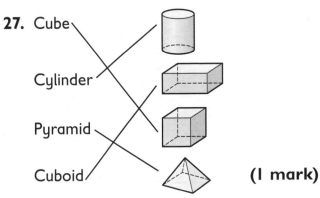

(1 mark)

28. 5 pieces   (1 mark)

29. 6 packs   (1 mark)

30. Vertices marked as shown:

(1 mark)

31.

(1 mark)

Set B Paper 1

Practice question   12

1.	100	(1 mark)
2.	15	(1 mark)
3.	19	(1 mark)
4.	10	(1 mark)
5.	14	(1 mark)
6.	9	(1 mark)

7. 40 + [60] = 100   (1 mark: both
     100 = 60 + [40]   correct for 1 mark)

8.	7	(1 mark)
9.	100	(1 mark)
10.	10	(1 mark)
11.	25	(1 mark)
12.	31	(1 mark)
13.	20	(1 mark)
14.	10	(1 mark)
15.	5	(1 mark)
16.	0	(1 mark)
17.	30	(1 mark)
18.	17	(1 mark)
19.	75	(1 mark)
20.	30	(1 mark)
21.	42	(1 mark)

22.	25	(1 mark)
23.	40	(1 mark)
24.	22	(1 mark)
25.	2	(1 mark)

Set B Paper 2

Practice question   50 stickers

1. Accept 307 *or* three hundred and seven

                                     (1 mark)

2.	May	(1 mark)
3.	13	(1 mark)
4.	6 faces	(1 mark)
5.	(2 hours)	(1 mark)
6.	2 metres ☑	(1 mark)

7.

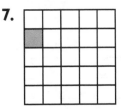

(1 mark)

8. 19   (1 mark)

9. *Any 2 **different** combinations of available coins that equal 56p, e.g.* 50p + 5p + 1p

10p + 10p + 20p + 5p + 5p + 2p + 2p + 2p

or other variants.

***Do not** accept multiples of coins that are **not** available, or amounts not represented by actual coins, e.g.*

50p + 6p *(A 6p coin does not exist)*
20p + 20p + 10p + 5p + 1p *(Only 1 × 20p is available)*

     (2 marks: 1 mark for each correct combination)

10. *Any number from 81–99 inclusive.*   **(1 mark)**

11. 13 balloons

     Any viable method shown, e.g.

     20 + 17 = 37   50 – 37 = 13

     or

     50 – 30 = 20   20 – 7 = 13

     (2 marks for correct answer. Award 1 mark for using appropriate method but wrong answer given.)

12.

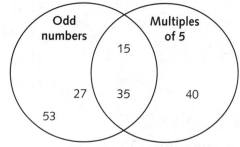

(2 marks: 1 mark for one of the circles correctly completed)

13. 30 **(1 mark)**

14. 65p **(1 mark)**

15. Cylinders have 2 circular faces. ☑

Cylinders do not have right-angle vertices. ☑ **(1 mark)**

16.

Bird	Tally	Total
Robin	IIII	4
Finch	IIII IIII I	11
Pigeon	IIII	5
Starling	IIII IIII II	12
Thrush	IIII III	8

(1 mark)

17. **(1 mark)**

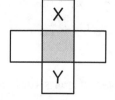

18. *Any suitable answers, e.g.*

$\frac{3}{3}$ = 1 whole

$\frac{2}{4}$ = $\frac{1}{2}$ or half

$\frac{3}{2}$ = $1\frac{1}{2}$ or one-and-a-half **(1 mark)**

19. 11 jugs **(1 mark)**

20.

(1 mark)

21.

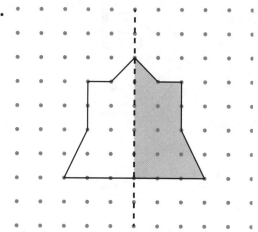

Reflective drawing shows understanding – accuracy may not be totally correct, but drawing shows concept. **(1 mark)**

22. 87 ⟶ 97

23 ⟶ 33

47 ⟶ 57

64 ⟶ 74

(1 mark)

23. 350 g **(1 mark)**

24. a) b)

(2 marks: 1 mark for each correct clock)

25. 14 packets

Any viable method shown, e.g.

7 × 2 = 14

2 + 2 + 2 + 2 + 2 + 2 + 2 = 14

(2 marks for correct answer. Award 1 mark for using appropriate method but wrong answer given.)

26. 10 crayons. *Also accept 9 or 11.* **(1 mark)**

27. £1.50 **(1 mark)**

28.

○ △ △ **(1 mark)**

29. A 10 cm line drawn correctly with a ruler. **(1 mark)**

30.

81 ──take away 10──▶ **71**

46 ──take away 10──▶ **36**

97 ──take away 10──▶ **87**

(1 mark)

Set C Paper 1

Practice question   6

1. 3 (1 mark)
2. 12 (1 mark)
3. 6 (1 mark)
4. 26 (1 mark)
5. 6 (1 mark)
6. 6 (1 mark)
7. 52 (1 mark)
8. 42 (1 mark)
9. 28 (1 mark)
10. 7 (1 mark)
11. 10 (1 mark)
12. $\boxed{55}$ − 12 = 43

    43 + 12 = $\boxed{55}$

    (1 mark: both correct for 1 mark)
13. 5 (1 mark)
14. 24 ÷ $\boxed{2}$ = 12

    $\boxed{12}$ × 2 = 24

    (1 mark: both correct for 1 mark)
15. 12 (1 mark)
16. 25 (1 mark)
17. 24 (1 mark)
18. 6 (1 mark)
19. 61 (1 mark)
20. 25 (1 mark)
21. 30 (1 mark)
22. 20 ÷ $\boxed{5}$ = 4

    $\boxed{5}$ × 4 = 20

    (1 mark: both correct for 1 mark)
23. 31 (1 mark)
24. 33 (1 mark)
25. 5 (1 mark)

Set C Paper 2

Practice question   15

1. 50p   20p   2p

   in any order (1 mark)
2. 41 (1 mark)
3. 11 children (1 mark)
4. 8 vertices (1 mark)
5. (centimetres) (1 mark)
6. 15 + 15 = 30 (1 mark)
7. 48 satsumas (1 mark)
8.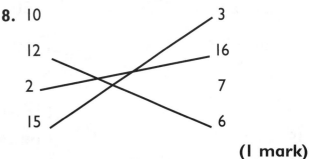

   (1 mark)
9. 500 g (1 mark)
10. *Accept:*

    10 lots of 5

    5 + 5 + 5 + 5 + 5 + 5 + 5 + 5 + 5 + 5

    10 × 5

    or any drawn answer that clearly relates to 10 groups of 5. (1 mark)
11. a)

15	18	21	24	27

    (1 mark)

    b)

55	50	45	40	35

    (1 mark)
12. $\dfrac{1}{3}$ or $\dfrac{2}{6}$ (1 mark)
13. (22°C) (1 mark)
14. a) 3 children (1 mark)

    b) Light brown (1 mark)
15. (0°C) (1 mark)

16.

(2 marks: 1 mark for each correct row)

17. 45 minutes (1 mark)

18.

(1 mark)

19. 15 (1 mark)

20. (1 mark)

21.

(1 mark)

22. Any combination of available coins that total 87p, e.g. 50p, 20p, 10p, 5p, 2p.

Do not accept multiples of coins that are **not** available or amounts not represented by actual coins. (1 mark)

23. ⟨2 litres⟩ (1 mark)

24. These grid references shaded.

5				
4		▨		
3				▨
2				
1			▨	

A B C D E

(1 mark)

25. 9 weeks (1 mark)

26. a) $8 \times 10 = 94 - \boxed{14}$ (1 mark)

b) $50 \div 5 = 2 \times \boxed{5}$ (1 mark)

27. 4 children (1 mark)

28. Any 4 extra squares shaded. (1 mark)

29.

523

497

481

458

410

(1 mark)

30. a)

Weather in March

Weather	Tally	Total
Sunny	卌	5
Showers	卌 |||	8
Cloudy	卌 卌	10
Rain	卌	5
Snow	|||	3

(1 mark)

b) Showers column shows 8 and Rain column shows 5:

Note: It is important that the graph shows an understanding of each block representing 2 items and a split block counting as 1. (1 mark)

Aural questions administration

The instructions below are for the first five questions in each Paper 2.

Explain to your child that the first question is a practice question. When reading the question, remember to repeat the bold text in the question. Before proceeding to question 1, ensure that your child knows where they should have written their answer and discuss with them how they worked out their answer. Allow them to change their answer to the correct one by crossing out or rubbing out, to make sure they know the way to correct errors.

Before reading out questions 1 to 5, tell your child that they should try to answer all of the questions. If they can't answer a question, they should move on to the next one and come back to that one later. Remind your child that you can't help answer these next questions and that they should try to work them out on their own. Read questions 1 to 5, allowing time for your child to write their answers. When reading the question, remember to repeat the bold text in the question. At the end of each question, allow sufficient time for your child to complete what they can.

Set A Paper 2

Read out these questions to your child. Explain that they should listen carefully and write their answers on pages 18–19.

Practice question

This is a practice question for us to do together.

Amy has 12 caterpillars. **Look at the caterpillars. Circle half of the caterpillars.**

1. Question 1. **What number is 8 less than 27?** Write your answer in the box.

2. Question 2. **There are 5 packs of stickers. Each pack has 5 stickers. How many stickers are there altogether?** Write your answer in the box.

3. Question 3. Emma's baby sister has just been born. **Circle the weight that you think Emma's baby sister is most likely to be.**

4. Question 4. **A banana costs 15p. How much money would 3 bananas cost?** Write your answer in the box.

5. Question 5. Look at the shapes. **Two of the shapes are pentagons. Tick (✓) the shapes that are pentagons.**

Set B Paper 2

Read out these questions to your child. Explain that they should listen carefully and write their answers on pages 46–47.

Practice question

This is a practice question for us to do together.

One pack has 10 stickers. How many stickers would there be in 5 packs? Write your answer in the box.

1 Question 1. **Write the number three hundred and seven.** Write your answer in the box.

2 Question 2. **February is the second month of the year. What is the fifth month?** Write your answer in the box.

3 Question 3. **What is the difference between 58 and 45?** Write your answer in the box.

4 Question 4. **A cuboid has how many faces?** Write your answer in the box.

5 Question 5. **Alba watches her favourite film. How long will the film probably last?** Circle the time that is most likely.

Set C Paper 2

Read out these questions to your child. Explain that they should listen carefully and write their answers on pages 74–75.

Practice question

This is a practice question for us to do together.

Here is a number sequence. What number would be next in this sequence? Write your answer in the box.

1 Question 1. **Hannah has 3 coins which total 72p. Which 3 coins must Hannah have?** Write your answer in the boxes.

2 Question 2. **What is 12 less than 53?** Write your answer in the box.

3 Question 3. **There are 5 children on a bus. At the next stop 9 more children get on and 3 children get off.**

How many children are left on the bus? Write your answer in the box.

4 Question 4. **A cube has 6 faces. How many vertices does it have?** Write your answer in the box.

5 Question 5. **Max needs to know how tall he is. Which standard units will he use?** Circle the correct standard unit used to measure length and height.

KS1 ENGLISH

SATs SUCCESS

PRACTICE TEST PAPERS

Ages 6–7

KS1 ENGLISH SATs

complete tests

PRACTICE TEST PAPERS

RACHEL GRANT

Contents

(pull-out section at the back of the book)

Introduction and instructions

How these tests will help your child

This book is made up of two sets of practice test papers. Each set contains similar test papers to those that your child will take in English reading and English grammar, punctuation and spelling at the end of Year 2. The tests will assess your child's knowledge, skills and understanding in the areas of study undertaken since they began Year 1. These practice test papers can be used any time throughout the year to provide practice for the Key Stage 1 tests.

The results of both sets of papers will provide a good idea of the strengths and weaknesses of your child.

Administering the tests

Provide your child with a quiet environment where they can complete each test undisturbed.

Provide your child with a pen or pencil, ruler and eraser.

The amount of time given for each test varies, so remind your child at the start of each one how long they have and give them access to a clock or watch.

You should only read the instructions out to your child, not the actual questions (except where instructed otherwise).

Although handwriting is not assessed, remind your child that their answers should be clear.

Advise your child that if they are unable to do one of the questions, they should to go on to the next one and come back to it later, if they have time. If they finish before the end, they should go back and check their work.

English reading

Paper 1: reading prompt and answer booklet

Each test is made up of an answer booklet containing two different reading prompts and questions.

All answers are worth 1 mark, with a total number of 20 marks for each test.

Your child will have approximately **30 minutes** to read the prompts and answer the questions.

Read the list of useful words and discuss their meanings with your child.

Read the practice questions out loud to your child and allow them time to write down their own answer.

Your child should read and answer the other questions by themselves.

Paper 2: reading answer booklet

Each test is made up of two different texts and an answer booklet.

All answers are worth 1 mark (unless otherwise stated), with a total number of 20 marks for each test.

Your child will have approximately **40 minutes** to read the texts in the reading booklet and answer the questions in the answer booklet.

English grammar, punctuation and spelling

Paper 1: spelling

- Contains 20 spellings, with each spelling worth 1 mark.
  Your child will have approximately **15 minutes** to complete the test paper.
- Using the spelling administration guide on pages 103–104, read each spelling and allow your child time to fill it in on their spelling paper.

Paper 2: questions

- All answers are worth 1 mark (unless otherwise stated), with a total number of 20 marks for each test.
- Your child will have approximately **20 minutes** to complete the test paper.
- Read the practice questions out loud to your child and allow them time to write down their own answer.
- Some questions are multiple choice and may require a tick in the box next to the answer. Some require a word or phrase to be underlined or circled while others have a line or box for the answer. Some questions ask for missing punctuation marks to be inserted.

Marking the practice test papers

The answers and mark scheme have been provided to enable you to check how your child has performed. Fill in the marks that your child achieved for each part of the tests.

Please note: these tests are **only a guide** to the mark your child can achieve and cannot guarantee the same is achieved during the Key Stage 1 tests, as the mark needed to achieve the expected standard varies from year to yea

English reading

	Set A	Set B
Paper 1: reading prompt and answer booklet	/20	/20
Paper 2: reading answer booklet	/20	/20
Total	/40	/40

The scores achieved on these practice test papers will help to show if your child is working at the expected standard in English reading:

11–20 = working towards the expected standard
21–30 = working at the expected standard
31–40 = working above the expected standard.

English grammar, punctuation and spelling

	Set A	Set B
Paper 1: spelling	/20	/20
Paper 2: questions	/20	/20
Total	/40	/40

The scores achieved on these practice test papers will help to show if your child is working at the expected standard in English grammar, punctuation and spelling:

11–20 = working towards the expected standard
21–30 = working at the expected standard
31–40 = working above the expected standard.

When an area of weakness has been identified, it is useful to go over these, and similar types of questions, with your child. Sometimes your child will be familiar with the subject matter but might not understand what the question is asking. This will become apparent when talking to your child.

Shared marking and target setting

Engaging your child in the marking process will help them to develop a greater understanding of the tests and, more importantly, provide them with some ownership of their learning. They will be able to see more clearly how and why certain areas have been identified for them to target for improvement.

Top tips for your child

Don't make silly mistakes. Make sure you emphasise to your child the importance of reading the question. Easy marks can be picked up by just doing as the question asks.

Make answers clearly legible. If your child has made a mistake, encourage them to put a cross through it and write the correct answer clearly next to it. Try to encourage your child to use an eraser as little as possible.

Don't panic! These practice test papers, and indeed the Key Stage 1 tests, are meant to provide a guide to the standard a child has attained. They are not the be-all and end-all, as children are assessed regularly throughout the school year. Explain to your child that there is no need to worry if they cannot do a question – tell them to g on to the next question and come back to the problematic question later if they have time.

Key Stage 1

English reading

Paper 1: reading prompt and answer booklet

Time:

You have approximately **30 minutes** to complete this test paper.

Maximum mark	Actual mark
20	

First name	
Last name	

2018 Letts Educational, an imprint of HarperCollinsPublishers Ltd – not to be photocopied.

5

Useful words

lighthouse

souvenir

The Story of Grace Darling

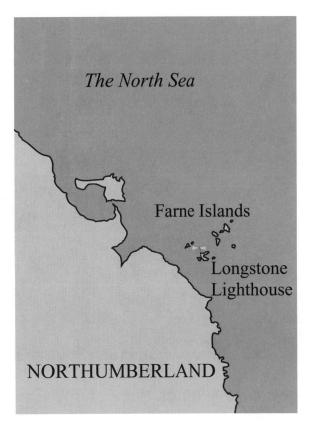

Grace Darling was a lighthouse keeper's daughter. She lived in Longstone lighthouse, which is in Northumberland in north-east England.

---

ractice questions

a Who was Grace Darling?

_____

b **Find** and **copy** the name of the lighthouse where Grace Darling lived.

_____

The lighthouse is on an island. Only Grace's family lived on the island.

Grace's father had an important job. He kept the light burning in the lighthouse.

The light warned ships about dangerous rocks in the sea.

---

1 What did Grace's father do?

_____ ◯

2 Which word in the text describes what the rocks were like?

Tick **one**.

lonely ☐   important ☐

dangerous ☐   burning ☐   ◯

© 2018 Letts Educational, an imprint of HarperCollinsPublishers Ltd – not to be photocopie n 7 September 1838 there was a big storm.

ship was passing Little Farne Island. It had 63 people on board.

uddenly, the engine stopped. The crew could not use the sails because of

e storm.

he ship drifted and hit the rocks.

---

3 How many people were on board the ship?

Tick **one**.

7 ☐   63 ☐

18 ☐   38 ☐

○

4 Give **two** reasons why the ship drifted and hit the rocks.

1. _____

2. _____   ○

Grace Darling saw the accident. She told her father about it. They did not think anyone on the ship would be alive.

When the sun rose, they saw people clinging to the rocks. Some people were still alive!

---

5 What did Grace do when she saw the accident?

_____ ◯

6 What did Grace and her father see when the sun rose?

_____ ◯

race and her father took their tiny rowing boat. They rowed through the
ormy sea, in winds and rain. They found nine people on the rocks. Grace kept
ontrol of the boat while her father went to help.

One by one, they helped the people into the boat. They rowed them to safety.

7 **Find** and **copy one** word that tells you what the sea was like.

_____

◯

8 Number the pictures 1 to 4 to show the order they happened in the story.

The first one has been done for you.

◯

2018 Letts Educational, an imprint of HarperCollinsPublishers Ltd – not to be photocopied.

11

When people heard Grace Darling's story, she became a national hero. Even Queen Victoria heard the story. Grace was given a silver medal.

Poems and songs were written about Grace. Souvenirs such as postcards and mugs with pictures of Grace on them were made.

---

9 Why did Grace become a national hero?

Tick **one**.

People wrote songs about Grace. ☐

People thought Grace was very brave. ☐

Grace's picture was on postcards. ☐

Queen Victoria heard Grace's story. ☐

○

Useful words

direction

thousands

13

Why Owls have Big Eyes

Owl and Pigeon were friends. They liked to meet at dawn and watch the sunrise. They liked to talk about many things.

One morning, Owl said to Pigeon, "There are more owls than pigeons."

"Nonsense!" said Pigeon. "There are lots more pigeons than owls!"

Practice questions

c *They liked to meet at dawn and watch the sunrise.*

What does *at dawn* mean in this sentence?

Tick **one**.

get together ☐ at home ☐

early in the morning ☐ in the woods ☐

d What did Owl say to Pigeon?

"There are _____ "

"There's only one way to find out," hooted Owl. "We will count them!"

"All right," cooed Pigeon. "Where shall we do it? We need a big place."

Owl thought for a minute and then he said, "The Big Wood has lots of trees."

'Fine," said Pigeon. "You tell the owls and I'll tell the pigeons. One week from today we will count them."

They both flew off to tell everyone.

10 Why was the Big Wood a good place to count the owls and pigeons?

_____ ◯

11 When did they decide they would count the owls and pigeons?

Tick **one**.

in two weeks	☐	today	☐
later this week	☐	in one week	☐

◯

One week later, the owls arrived at the Big Wood, just as the sun rose.

They flew down from every direction until the trees were full.

They laughed and said, "Too-woo, wah, wah! The pigeons are still asleep!"

They were sure there could not be as many pigeons.

---

12 How do you know there were a lot of owls in the Big Wood?

_____ ◯

13 *They were sure there could not be as many pigeons.*

What does the word *sure* mean in this sentence?

Tick **one**.

certain ☐   safe ☐

trust ☐   truthful ☐ ◯

After a while they saw huge grey clouds moving towards them. The clouds were pigeon wings.

Thousands of pigeons flew down to the Big Wood and as they landed, the owls moved closer together. Branches broke when too many pigeons tried to land at once.

The owls' eyes grew wider and wider as they tried to see all the pigeons. They stared and moved their heads from side to side to watch the pigeons.

14 **Find** and **copy two** words that tell you what the clouds really were.

_____ ◯

15 Why did the owls move closer together?

Tick **one**.

To laugh at the pigeons. ☐ To make room for the pigeons. ☐

To watch the pigeons. ☐ To welcome the pigeons. ☐ ◯

The pigeons kept coming. The owls could not believe there were so many pigeons!

The owls started to feel nervous and hooted, "Tooooo-woooo! Let's get out of here!"

One by one the owls flew away, up between the branches.

---

16 Why did the owls decide to fly away?

Tick **two**.

It was getting late. ☐   They felt cold. ☐

They felt nervous. ☐   There was no room for them. ☐ ◯

17 Number the sentences below from 1 to 4 to show the order they happen in the story.

The first one has been done for you.

The owls flew off. ☐   The owls became worried. ☐

More pigeons arrived. ☐ 1   The owls were surprised. ☐ ◯

wl and Pigeon never did count how many owls and pigeons there were.

low the owls always fly at night so that they will not meet pigeons.

heir eyes are big and round and they stare because they are looking out

or pigeons.

18 Do you think there were more pigeons than owls?

Tick **one**.

Yes ☐   No ☐

Give one reason for your answer.

_____ ◯

19 Give **two** things that owls do now because of the pigeons.

1. _____

2. _____ ◯

20 Think about all you have read.

How do you think the pigeons felt after the owls flew away, and why?

_____

_____

◯

Key Stage 1

English reading

Paper 2: reading answer booklet

Time:

You have approximately **40 minutes** to read the texts in the reading booklet (pages 82–87) and answer the questions in the answer booklet.

Maximum mark	Actual mark
20	

First name	
Last name	

(page 82)

1 Why did Anansi want to taste the food that his neighbours cooked?

_____

(page 82)

2 *they were stubby, but strong.*

What does the word *stubby* mean?

Tick **one**.

black and hairy ☐

short and thick ☐

long and thin ☐

tired and weak ☐

(page 82)

3 Why didn't Anansi wait at Rabbit's house?

_____

(page 83)

4 What was Fox cooking for his family?

_____

(page 83)

5 At Monkey's house, why did Anansi tie his leg to the oven door?

_____ ◯

(page 84)

6 **a)** Draw **four** lines to match these characters to the foods they were cooking.

Elephant	●	● nut roast
Squirrel	●	● chicken curry
Giraffe	●	● rice pudding
Hog	●	● honey cake

◯

b) What did each of the animals promise to do when dinner was ready?

_____ ◯

7 **Find** and **copy** the **three** words that show that Anansi was looking forward to having eight dinners.

_____

8 Number the sentences below from 1 to 4 to show the order in which they happened.

The first one has been done for you.

The river washed the webs away. ☐

Rabbit tugged a web. ☐

Anansi talked to Fox. ☐ 1

Anansi's legs started to grow long and skinny. ☐

(page 86)

9 Water is needed for...

Tick **two**.

washing our clothes. ☐

burning wood. ☐

plants to grow. ☐

drying our clothes. ☐

○

(page 86)

10 Look at the section headed: **The Water Cycle**

Find and **copy** the word that means the same as *small drops*.

_____ ○

(page 86)

11 What does the word *cycle* mean in *the water cycle*?

_____

_____ ○

12 Copy the two labels into the correct boxes on either side of the diagram.

| water changes from liquid into gas | | water falls as rain, hail, snow or sleet |

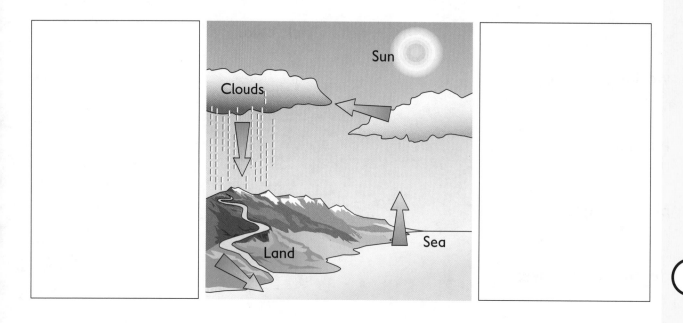

13 What happens to water when the sun heats it up?

_____

_____

14 Look at the section: **FACT FILE**

Find and **copy** how much water you have in your:

1. blood _____

2. skin _____ ◯

15 Look at the section: **What is Polluted Water?**

Give **three** things that can cause water pollution.

1. _____

2. _____

3. _____ ◯

16 **Find** and **copy two** words that mean the same as *rubbish*.

1. _____

2. _____

17 Why is water precious?

Give **one** reason.

_____

18 Put ticks in the table to show which sentences are **true** and which are **false**.

One has been done for you.

The information says that...	True	False
humans cause all polluted water.		✓
we should try to save water.		
90% of the world's water is not fresh.		
you should pick up your litter, but only when you are at a beach, lake or river.		
a watering can uses less water than a hosepipe.		

2 marks

END OF TEST

English grammar, punctuation and spelling

Paper 1: spelling

You will need to ask someone to read the instructions and sentences to you. These can be found on page 103.

Time:

You have approximately **15 minutes** to complete this test paper.

Maximum mark	Actual mark
20	....

First name	
Last name	

2018 Letts Educational, an imprint of HarperCollins Publishers Ltd – not to be photocopied.

29

Spelling

Practice question

The children _____ in the park.

---

1. The ice is too thin to _____ on.   ◯

2. Our cat has long _____.   ◯

3. An elephant's nose is called a _____.   ◯

4. Sit in the chair _____ the door.   ◯

5. Sally found a magpie _____.   ◯

6. Please give me your _____ number.   ◯

7. We all enjoyed the cricket _____.   ◯

8. Dad _____ Milly's pram.   ◯

9. We are going swimming on _____.   ◯

10. We build a _____ on the beach.   ◯

1. Hannah has _____ to do today.

2. My _____ loves playing football.

3. You wear a watch on your _____.

4. The hat is _____ with yellow flowers.

5. I do not want to _____ with you.

6. Please pass me the pink _____.

7. This fish is very _____.

8. Plastic is a _____ material.

9. Our school has a _____ in September.

0. Alex gave me an _____ to his party.

END OF SPELLING TEST

Key Stage 1

English grammar, punctuation and spelling

Paper 2: questions

Time:

You have approximately **20 minutes** to complete this test paper.

Maximum mark	Actual mark
20	

First name	
Last name	

ractice questions

a Write one word on the line to complete the sentence in the present tense.

Sally is _____ **a book.**

b Tick the correct punctuation mark to complete the sentence.

Where do you live

Tick **one**.

full stop ☐

question mark ☐

exclamation mark ☐

comma ☐

1 Circle **three** words that should have a capital letter in the sentences below.

it is a hot day. sally and tom are eating ice cream.

2 Tick the correct word to complete the sentence below.

Do you prefer orange juice _____ apple juice?

and ☐

or ☐

but ☐

so ☐

3 Tick the phrase that uses the correct punctuation to complete the sentence below.

Where are you going _____

Tick **one**.

on holiday this year! ☐

on holiday this year. ☐

on holiday this year ☐

on holiday this year? ☐

4 Tick the punctuation mark that should complete each sentence.

Sentence	Full stop	Question mark
You can have tea at our house		
Are you coming to play football		
Where are my shoes		
It is lunchtime now		

5 What type of word is underlined in the sentence below?

Meera carefully picked up the fluffy <u>hamster</u>.

Tick **one**.

a verb ☐

a noun ☐

an adjective ☐

an adverb ☐

6 Write the missing punctuation mark to complete the sentence below.

What a wonderful surprise it was

○

7 Read the sentences below.

Last week, we went to the seaside.

We took our buckets and spades and we packed a picnic.

We played on the sandy beach and in the rock pools.

Then we paddled in the warm sea.

Tick the word that best describes these sentences.

Tick **one**.

questions ☐

commands ☐

exclamations ☐

statements ☐

○

8 Circle the **four** nouns in the sentence below.

Green plants need air, water and sunlight to grow.

◯

9 Which word correctly completes the sentence?

Brett felt _____ when he lost his favourite toy.

Tick **one**.

happy ☐

inhappy ☐

unhappy ☐

imhappy ☐

◯

10 Underline the **two** adjectives in the sentence below.

In the garden, a cheeky robin hopped onto a branch and he sang a sweet song.

○

11 Write **ful** or **less** to complete the word in each sentence.

Did you see that colour_____ rainbow in the sky?

The fear_____ explorer went bravely into the jungle.

○

12 What type of word is underlined in the sentence below?

The fat ginger cat gazed <u>hungrily</u> at the bright blue fish darting in the water.

an adverb ☐

a noun ☐

an adjective ☐

a verb ☐

○

13 Write **three** commas in the correct places in the sentence below.

You must bring a coat gloves a hat boots and a packed lunch to school on Friday.

○

14 The verb in the box is in the present tense.

Write the **past tense** of the verb in the space.

$$\boxed{\text{runs}}$$
↓

Aisha's mum _____ very fast in the egg and spoon race.

  ◯

15 Why does the underlined word have an apostrophe?

Put your books on the <u>teacher's</u> desk.

_____

_____

  ◯

16 Write **was** or **were** to complete the sentence below correctly.

The birds _____ flying high up in the sky.

  ◯

17 Yusuf and Brandon are at the zoo. They are looking at the parrots. Brandon wants to give the parrots some of his sandwich. Yusuf wants to stop him.

Write the words that Yusuf says to Brandon in the speech bubble.

Remember to use the correct punctuation.

2 marks

18 The verbs that are underlined are in the present tense.

Write these verbs in the **past tense**.

One has been done for you.

Hari <u>bakes</u> a cake for my birthday.

Hari <u>baked</u> a cake for my birthday.

He <u>uses</u> flour, butter, eggs and sugar.

He _____ flour, butter, eggs and sugar.

I <u>choose</u> the chocolate icing and cherries to go on top.

I _____ the chocolate icing and cherries

to go on top.

2 marks

END OF TEST

2018 Letts Educational, an imprint of HarperCollinsPublishers Ltd – not to be photocopied.

43

Key Stage 1

English reading

Paper 1: reading prompt and answer booklet

Time:

You have approximately **30 minutes** to complete this test paper.

Maximum mark	Actual mark
20	....

First name	
Last name	

Useful words

mainland

million

2018 Letts Educational, an imprint of HarperCollinsPublishers Ltd – not to be photocopied.

45

Two Countries

Greece

Greece is a country in the south-east of Europe.

It has a mainland, which has many mountains, and about 3000 small islands.

Practice questions

a Where is Greece?

_____

b **Find** and **copy two** things that you can find in Greece.

1. _____

2. _____

Wales has sea
on three
of its sides

ENGLAND

WALES

Wales

Wales is a country in the north-west of Europe. It is part of the United Kingdom.

Wales has 138 mountains and lots of valleys. The longest river in the United

Kingdom is called the River Severn. It begins in Wales.

---

1 What is Wales part of?

Tick **one**.

The Severn ☐   The United Kingdom ☐

England ☐   The River Severn ☐ ◯

2 **Find** and **copy** the name of the country that joins on to Wales.

_____ ◯

Greece and Wales

These are some differences between Greece and Wales.

	Greece	**Wales**
Weather in the summer	Usually very hot	Usually cool but sometimes hot
Islands	About 3000	About 50
Highest mountain	Mount Olympus	Mount Snowdon
Capital city	Athens	Cardiff
Population	11 million	3 million
Flag		

3 Tick **two** statements that are **true**.

Greece has more people than Wales. ☐

Wales has more islands than Greece. ☐

Greece's capital city is Athens. ☐

Mount Olympus is the highest mountain in Wales. ☐

4 Write **one** reason why Greece is a popular place to go on holiday.

_____ ◯

5 Which word in the text means the same as *all the people who live in a country?*

Tick **one**.

flag ☐

population ☐

capital ☐

million ☐ ◯

Useful words

vanished

electricity

Special Shoes

nce upon a time, not long ago, in a small
lage there lived a little girl called Lena.

e lived with her mum, her dad and her
der sister Maya. Maya liked running,
ncing, hopscotch and rounders. Lena
ed gardening, drawing and reading
venture stories.

actice questions

c Where did Lena live?

_____

d Tick to show the things that Lena and Maya liked.

One has been done for you.

	Lena liked	Maya liked
rounders		✓
hopscotch		
reading		
drawing		
dancing		

It was a hot day in July, and Lena and her sister Maya went out to pick raspberries. Soon, Maya decided she was bored with picking. She lay down on the grass and went to sleep.

"Lazybones," said Lena. "I can pick enough raspberries by myself. Mum will be pleased and we can eat them with cream for our tea."

---

6 Why did Lena say "Lazybones"?

Tick **one**.

because Lena was lazy ☐

because Lena was tired ☐

because Lena thought Maya was lazy ☐

because Lena thought Maya was tired ☐

7 Why did Lena want to pick the raspberries by herself? Give **two** reasons.

1. _____

2. _____

ll of a sudden, a little old lady appeared

om nowhere.

e was carrying a basket.

Hello Lena," said the old lady. "It's your

cky day!"

How do you know my name?" asked

na, surprised. "Why is today lucky?"

Aha!" said the old lady. "That's for me to

now, and for you to find out."

---

8 Where did the old lady appear from?

_____ ◯

9 What did the old lady say that surprised Lena the most?

Tick **one**.

"It's your lucky day!" ☐

"Aha!" ☐

"That's for me to know, and for you to find out." ☐

"Hello Lena." ☐ ◯

Lena was curious. "How can I find out?" she asked.

"I see you have some fine raspberries there," said the old lady. "I am very hungry, so here's what I will do. If you give me those raspberries that you have picked, I will give you this shoe box."

"Shoes?" said Lena. "I already have a pair of shoes, thank you very much!"

"Yes," said the old lady, "but not like these. These shoes are special. You'll see!"

---

10 Which word tells you how Lena felt about the old lady?

Tick **one**.

curious	☐	frightened	☐
annoyed	☐	hungry	☐

11 What did the old lady say was inside the shoe box?

_____

o Lena gave the old lady the raspberries, and she took the shoe box.

he gasped when she opened the box. Inside were the most beautiful shoes

he had ever seen.

hey were bright green with bows. The soles were clean and shiny.

Can I put them on?" she asked the old lady.

ut the old lady had vanished.

---

12 How do you know that Lena was surprised when she opened the box?

_____ ◯

13 How can you tell that the shoes were brand new?

_____ ◯

14 What happened to the old lady?

_____ ◯

Lena put the shoes on her feet. To her surprise, they fitted perfectly. As she stood up, she felt a shivery feeling, like icy electricity. It went through her legs and her body, right up to the top of her head. Her hair seemed to stand on end.

How strange! she thought.

"Time to go home!" she called. She poked Maya. "Wakey-wakey, Lazybones!"

---

15 *As she stood up, she felt a shivery feeling, like icy electricity.*

What does the word *shivery* mean in this sentence?

Tick **one**.

warm ☐   very cold ☐

hot ☐   very hot ☐   ◯

16 How did Lena feel when she put on the shoes?

Tick **one**.

tired ☐   surprised ☐

bored ☐   upset ☐   ◯

17 What did Lena do to wake Maya up?

_____   ◯

"Where are the raspberries?" said Maya.

"You were a lazybones," said Lena, "so there aren't any."

"You ate them all!" said Maya. "Wait until I tell Mum!"

"Pooh! I bet I get home first!" said Lena, and she whooshed down the hill and zipped through the gate. Maya blinked and her mouth fell open.

Yowee! thought Lena, as she zoomed into the kitchen. These shoes *are* special! I wonder what *else* they can do?

---

18 How do you know that Maya felt amazed when Lena ran home?

_____

◯

19 What did Lena wonder when she reached the kitchen?

_____

◯

20 Number the sentences below from 1 to 4 to show the order they happened in the story.

The first one has been done for you.

Lena put the shoes on.   ☐

Lena met an old lady.   ☐

Lena's sister fell asleep.   1

Lena traded the raspberries for a shoe box.   ☐

END OF TEST

Key Stage 1

English reading

Paper 2: reading answer booklet

Time:

You have approximately **40 minutes** to read the texts in the reading booklet (pages 89–94) and answer the questions in the answer booklet.

Maximum mark	Actual mark
20	....

First name	
Last name	

(page 89)

1 How many types of honey bee are there?

_____

◯

(page 89)

2 Tick **two** things that are **true** about worker bees.

always female ☐

live for up to one year ☐

mate with the queen bee ☐

die after stinging ☐

◯

(page 90)

3 Why do worker bees do the waggle dance?

_____

◯

(page 90)

4 Look at the box: **The Bees need you!**

Give **two** reasons why there are fewer bees each year.

1. _____

2. _____

◯

5 Look at the section: **Why do we need Bees?**

Write **two** things that might happen if bees die out.

1. _____

2. _____

○

6 Look at the section: **Why do we need Bees?**

Find and **copy** the word that means the same as *very important*.

_____

○

7 Look at the section: **Pollination.**

Number the steps 1 to 4 to show how pollination works.

The first one has been done for you.

Pollen helps other flowers to make seeds.

☐

The bee moves to other flowers.

☐

The pollen rubs off the bee's body.

☐

Pollen from a flower sticks to the bee's body.

| 1 |

◯

8 Look at the section: **Make a Bee Garden.**

Draw **three** lines to match the words below to their meaning.

Words	Meanings
protect ●	● making flowers
habitats ●	● natural homes
flowering ●	● keep safe

◯

(page 92)

9 Who was Mrs Rose?

_____ ◯

(page 92)

10 Why was life in space lonely?

_____ ◯

(page 92)

11 How did Skylar, Zoe and Mrs Rose know something had happened?

_____ ◯

2018 Letts Educational, an imprint of HarperCollinsPublishers Ltd – not to be photocopied.

63

12 *It was the strangest little creature I had ever seen.*

What does the word *strangest* mean?

Tick **one**.

the most furry ☐

the most odd ☐

the most strong ☐

the most friendly ☐

13 How did Zoe feel about the alien?

_____

14 **Find** and **copy one** word that tells you how the alien was feeling.

_____

(page 93)

15 How do you know Skylar was not frightened of the alien? Give **two** things.

1. _____

2. _____

◯

(page 93)

16 Why couldn't they keep the alien?

◯

_____

(page 94)

17 a) Put ticks in the table to show which sentences are **true** and which ones are **false**.

The first one has been done for you.

The story says that Mr and Mrs Smik...	True	False
have five long sticks.		✓
have tentacles.		
have very little fur.		
have pale pink skin.		
have lumpy skin.		

◯

2 marks

b) What sort of creatures do you think Mr and Mrs Smik were?

◯

_____

(page 94)

18 Why did Skylar think dog-dog would be back some day?

_____

END OF TEST

Key Stage 1

English grammar, punctuation and spelling

Paper 1: spelling

You will need to ask someone to read the instructions and sentences to you. These can be found on pages 103–104.

Time:

You have approximately **15 minutes** to complete this test paper.

Maximum mark	Actual mark
20	

First name	
Last name	

Spelling

Practice question

The birds _____ into the sky.

---

1.   Gina shows great _____ on the piano.   ○

2.   The postman brought a big _____.   ○

3.   The eggs _____ under the hen.   ○

4.   Our new _____ loves to play with us.   ○

5.   The children had an amazing time at the _____.   ○

6.   The sky was _____ when we left home.   ○

7.   Tom _____ TV after he has done his homework.   ○

8.   Dad is _____ vegetables for dinner.   ○

9.   Gran is coming to tea on _____.   ○

10.   Jane was too _____ to join in our game.   ○

1. He thinks reading is _____ than writing. ◯

2. Eating fresh fruit every day is good for your _____ . ◯

3. The hot air balloon rose _____ the rooftops. ◯

4. She loves all vegetables, especially _____ . ◯

5. Mum _____ to answer the door. ◯

6. Jane _____ at school today. ◯

7. Uncle Toby took his _____ to the park. ◯

8. The river runs through a deep _____ . ◯

9. Yesterday I saw a _____ with seven spots. ◯

0. I enjoy reading stories with lots of _____ . ◯

END OF SPELLING TEST

Key Stage 1

English grammar, punctuation and spelling

Paper 2: questions

Time:

You have approximately **20 minutes** to complete this test paper.

Maximum mark	Actual mark
20	....

First name	
Last name	

ractice questions

a Tick the word that completes the sentence.

Gerbils are usually _____ **than hamsters.**

smallest ☐

small ☐

little ☐

smaller ☐

b Write the words **do not** as one word, using an apostrophe.

Please _____ **pick the flowers.**

2018 Letts Educational, an imprint of HarperCollinsPublishers Ltd – not to be photocopied.

71

1 Underline the **noun phrase** in the sentence.

Do you like my new green hat?

2 Circle **three** words that must have capital letters in the sentence.

My birthday is in april and jane's birthday is in may.

3 Tick the best option to complete the sentence.

Will you put the books away, please

full stop ☐

exclamation mark ☐

question mark ☐

comma ☐

4 Write the missing punctuation mark to complete the sentence below.

Our school trip is to Leeds Castle

◯

5 What type of word is <u>hurt</u> in the sentence below?

Shelley slipped on the ice and hurt her leg.

Tick **one**.

a noun ☐

an adjective ☐

an adverb ☐

a verb ☐

◯

2018 Letts Educational, an imprint of HarperCollinsPublishers Ltd – not to be photocopied.

73

6 Which sentence has the correct punctuation?

What a great idea I have ☐

What a great idea I have! ☐

What a great idea I have? ☐

What a great idea I have, ☐

7 Circle the **adverb** in the sentence below.

We all cheered loudly when my sister won the race.

8 Tick the word that completes the sentence.

They _____ **at a lovely hotel.**

Tick **one**.

stayed ☐

stays ☐

staying ☐

to stay ☐

◯

9 Tick to show whether each sentence is in the **present tense** or the **past tense.**

	Present tense	Past tense
I was talking to Mary.		
Jack is brushing his teeth.		

◯

2018 Letts Educational, an imprint of HarperCollinsPublishers Ltd – not to be photocopied.

75

10 Read the sentences below.

Oh no! The dog has chewed my trainers!

Tick the word that best describes the sentences.

statements ☐

exclamations ☐

commands ☐

questions ☐

11 Tick the sentence that is a **statement**.

Tick **one**.

How exciting! We're going on holiday! ☐

Have you got the tickets? ☐

Carry your suitcase to the car. ☐

I have locked the front door. ☐

12 Write **two** commas where they should go in the sentence below.

Spring summer autumn and winter are the four seasons of the year.

$\bigcirc$

13 Tick the sentence that is written correctly in the **past tense**.

Tick **one**.

We are going to the shop and buying some ice cream. ☐

We went to the shop and bought some ice cream. ☐

We go to the shop and bought some ice cream. ☐

We went to the shop and buy some ice cream. ☐ $\bigcirc$

14 Circle **two** adjectives in the sentence below.

When we woke up in the morning, the soft, white

snow was falling silently from the sky.

15 Write the words in the boxes as one word, using an **apostrophe**.

One has been done for you.

I'm building a sandcastle.

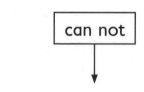

He _____ go swimming today.

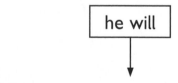

I hope _____ be better tomorrow.

2 marks

16 Tick **two** sentences that are correct.

They is closing the paddling pool. ☐

The park is closing soon. ☐

Peter is closing the door quietly. ☐

I are closing my eyes and counting to ten. ☐

○

17 Draw **four** lines to match the sentences with their correct type.

When we got home it was time for bed. ●	● question
Pass the salt. ●	● exclamation
When is it lunchtime? ●	● statement
How much I love it! ●	● command

○

18 Write **one** sentence to describe something in the picture.

Remember to use correct punctuation.

2 marks

_____

END OF TEST

SET
A

English
reading

PAPER 2:
READING
BOOKLET

Paper 2:
reading booklet

Why Spiders have Thin Legs

pages 82–85

Water

pages 86–87

Why Spiders have Thin Legs

Once upon a time, a long time ago, there lived a greedy spider named Anansi. Anansi loved his wife's cooking as she always cooked delicious food. Anansi also loved tasting the food that his neighbours cooked for themselves.

One day, Anansi was walking down the road on his short, thick legs. He had eight legs, and they were stubby, but strong. "I wonder what we are having for dinner," Anansi thought. "I hope it is beef stew! Yum yum. Beef stew is my favourite!"

Just then he smelled something delicious. The smell came from Rabbit's house. Rabbit was his good friend. "What's cooking?" asked Anansi. "I smell carrot soup!"

Rabbit came out of his house. He knew Anansi was greedy.

"You are welcome to some soup," said Rabbit, "but it is not ready. If you wait for a while, you can eat with me."

"Oh, no," said Anansi. "I'm sorry, Rabbit, but I can't wait because I am very busy." In fact, Anansi was lazy. He knew that Rabbit would give him jobs to do. Anansi didn't want to sweep the floor or wash dishes. He wanted to eat the carrot soup!

"I have an idea," said Anansi. "I will spin a web. I will tie one end around my leg and one end to your pot. When the soup is ready, you give the web a tug, and I will come back!"

"Good idea!" said Rabbit.

So Anansi spun a web. He tied one end to one of his legs. He tied the other end to the pot.

"See you later!" he said to Rabbit.

Moments later, Anansi smelled another delicious smell. This time it was beans and rice. His friend Fox was cooking a delicious meal for his family. Fox invited Anansi to stay but Anansi was afraid of the jobs he would need to do. He didn't want to do any work, so he tied another web to one of his legs. He tied the other end to the cooking pot.

"Please tug when the beans and rice are ready!" he said.

A few minutes later, Anansi's nose started to twitch. He smelled something delicious!

The smell came from Monkey's house.

"What is that delicious smell?" Anansi called.

"Banana bread!" said Monkey. "It's almost ready. Do you want to taste it?"

"I would love to," said Anansi.

And again, Anansi spun a web. He tied one end to his leg and the other end to the oven door. Monkey thought this was a great idea. He promised to tug on the web when the banana bread was ready.

Then Anansi went on his way.

At Elephant's house, he smelled sweet and creamy rice pudding. Rhino was cooking chops and greens. Squirrel was making a delicious nut roast. Giraffe was busy cooking a wonderful honey cake. Hog was making chicken curry for his family. Each one invited Anansi to stay to dinner. Each one promised to tug on a web when dinner was ready.

At last, Anansi was walking along with a web tied to each of his eight short legs. He was very pleased with himself. He was going to have eight dinners, and do no work at all! His mouth watered as he thought about the delicious meals waiting for him.

Just then, he felt a tug on one of his legs. "It's Rabbit!" cried Anansi.

"Great! Carrot soup!" He turned to go to Rabbit's house. Then he felt a tug on a different leg. Monkey's banana bread was ready!

"Oh dear!" said Anansi. Which dinner should he eat first? Then there was a tug on another leg, and then another. Soon, every one of Anansi's legs was being pulled at once.

"Help!" he cried. His legs were growing thinner and thinner!

What could he do? Just then he had an idea. He jumped as hard as he could, and landed in the river.

The river washed the webs away and his legs were free.

When he climbed out of the river, Anansi was very tired.

He looked down at his legs. They were thin and very long.

"Oh, my!" he said. "What will my wife say?"

He hurried home to dinner.

"What happened?" asked his wife. "Your legs are so long and skinny!"

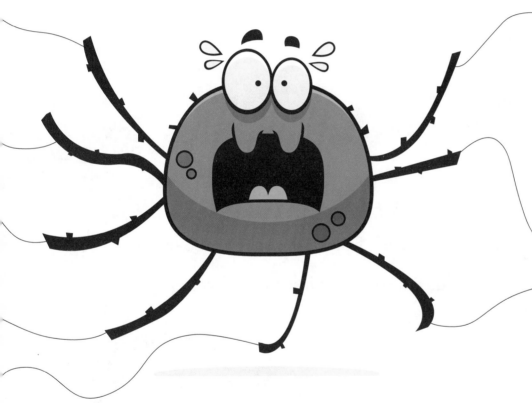

"Never mind," said Anansi. "I am very hungry. I need some beef stew!"

"You are too late," said his wife. "It's all gone."

So Anansi didn't eat any dinner that day. That is why he still visits
everyone's house, searching for food, with his eight thin legs.

Water

We use water every day. We drink water. We use it to wash our bodies, our clothes and our dishes.

Plants need water to grow and animals need it to live.

The Water Cycle

Water goes round and round, in a cycle. Cycle means a circle of events that happen again and again in the same order.

When the sun heats up water in seas and rivers, some of the water droplets move into the air.

The water changes from a liquid into a gas. Just like the water that comes out of a kettle when it boils!

The water droplets join up to make a cloud.

When the clouds get big and full of water, the water droplets fall from the sky. They may fall as rain or hail, snow or sleet, if it is very cold.

The water falls onto the land, sea and rivers. Or it falls on your umbrella, your roof or your head!

REMEMBER

The water cycle is always happening, all the time. Water is always turning from a liquid into a gas and back again. Clouds are always forming. There is always rain, hail, snow or sleet falling somewhere in the world.

Brain 70%

Blood 80%

Skin 70%

Water in the Body

Did you know that water makes up 70% of your body?

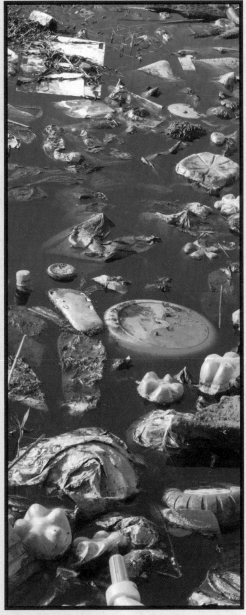

What is Polluted Water?

Polluted water is dirty water that is harmful to many living things.

Sometimes water becomes polluted because of things like storms, floods and animal waste. Some polluted water is caused by human activity. Food waste, chemicals such as oil, and refuse can cause water pollution.

Polluted water can make humans and other animals sick.

Only 1% of the world's water is fresh and safe to drink. The rest is salty and we can't drink it. Water is precious because we need it every day, so use it wisely.

What can you do to help?
* Always pick up your litter, especially when you are at a beach, lake or river.
* Save water by taking shorter showers, turning off taps and using a cup when you brush your teeth.
* Use a watering can (not a hosepipe) to water the garden.

SET
B

**English
reading**

**PAPER 2:
READING
BOOKLET**

Paper 2:
reading booklet

All about Bees

pages 89–91

Alien on Board

pages 92–94

All about Bees

Honey bees live in hives. There are three types of honey bees in the hive: the queen bee, the drones and the workers.

The **queen bee** lives between 1 and 4 years. She eats royal jelly that the worker bees provide. Her job is to lay eggs.

The **drones** are male bees. They mate with the queen to create more bees. They do not have a sting.

The **workers** are female bees. There may be as many as 60000 in one hive. Worker bees collect pollen and nectar, feed the drones, build and protect the hive, collect water and feed the eggs. If they use their sting, they die.

The Waggle Dance

If a worker bee finds flowers with a lot of nectar and pollen, she goes back to the hive. She moves in a figure of eight and waggles her body to show the other bees where the food is. This movement is called the waggle dance.

The Bees need you!

Bees have been disappearing from our country. Every year there are fewer bees. Some of the reasons for this are use of chemicals, loss of habitat, lack of food and poisons in the air.

Why do we need Bees?

Bees do essential work. They take pollen from plant to plant. This is called pollination. The plants need the pollen in order to grow new seeds. Without pollination, our flower, fruit, nut and vegetable plants would die.

Pollination

The flower is colourful and smells good!

It has nectar and pollen in it! Yum!

Yum yum! I have pollen on my body as well as in my mouth!

Oh yummy! The pollen from my body is helping this flower to make seeds!

Make a Bee Garden

We need to protect our bees by making wild habitats for them to live in.

Attract bees to your garden by planting flowers that bees like. They like wild flowers such as cornflowers, poppies, lavender, foxgloves and bluebells.

Fruit trees, herbs and flowering shrubs are also good.

Alien on Board

Our family lives on a spaceship. My dad is the captain of the ship and he's a Galaxy Map Maker. He makes maps of the galaxies we travel through. I'm Skylar and I'm 7 years old. My little sister Zoe and I have lived here all our lives. We live here alone – except for our teacher, Mrs Rose. I almost forgot Mrs Rose because she isn't really a person. She is a computer, but she is very lifelike, and very strict, just like all teachers.

Life in space can be very lonely. It's so quiet, and so dark, except for the stars. Sometimes I wish I had a friend, or that we could meet an alien, for company. But nothing ever happens. We've been travelling in space for years but we have never seen any aliens, monsters or scary creatures at all.

Then, last Tuesday, just as we were finishing our lessons with Mrs Rose, we heard a buzz and a loud CRASH! It came from the landing area. We rushed to see what had happened. There was a small, grey space shuttle, with an alien inside!

The alien looked at us. We looked at the alien. It was the strangest little creature I had ever seen. It was almost completely black, except for its nose, which was brown. It had brown stripes down both of its front legs and it had two eyes! Surely one eye is enough for anyone? And fur should be pink, like ours, not black!

"What on earth!?" said Dad.

"I don't like it!" said Zoe. "Make it go away!"

"Don't be silly," said Dad. "It's more frightened of you than you are of it."

He opened the shuttle door.

The alien crouched down. It looked terrified. Then it showed its teeth, huge and white.

I went up to the alien and knelt down.

"Don't be afraid," I said, gently. "We won't hurt you!"

"Be careful, Skylar!" said Dad.

"It's all right," I replied. "See. It's friendly."

The alien was shaking its bottom. A long, soft, furry stick-like thing made swooshing noises. A soft, pink, wet thing came out of its mouth and brushed against my ear.

"Aw!" I said. "It's cute! Can we keep it, Dad?"

Dad was looking at the shuttle. "Property of Mr and Mrs Smik. If found, please return to 92, The Hutchings, Planet Zogg," he read.

Zoe was petting the alien, "Cutie, cutie!"

"What sort of alien is it?" I asked Dad.

"It's not an alien," said Dad. "It's a dog. I wonder how it got here. We need to take it home."

"Dog-dog," said Zoe. "Nice dog-dog!"

"Oh!" I said. I was disappointed. Here was my first alien, and it wasn't an alien at all!

"You'd better take it to the main deck," said Dad. "I'll radio to Planet Zogg and speak to Mr and Mrs Smik."

Dog-dog followed us to the main deck.

"Do you think it likes moss cake?" I asked Zoe.

It was fun having dog-dog on the spaceship. First it ate some moss cake. Then it tried the fungus pie. After that it bounced on Zoe's space hopper. Finally, it jumped right onto the control panel and started pressing buttons.

"Stop that!" shouted Dad. "I'm flying this spaceship, not you! We're flying to Planet Zogg, right now!"

When we landed on Planet Zogg, dog-dog's owners were there to meet us. They looked every bit as strange as dog-dog. For a start, they had hardly any fur at all. Their skin was smooth and a pale pink colour all over. They had no tentacles, just four long sticks with five wriggly things at each end. Mr Smik had a patch of red hair just below his nose. Mrs Smik's mouth seemed to have something wrong with it. It was huge and red, like an exploded cherry.

"Darling!" said Mrs Smik. Her voice was squeaky and high.

Dog-dog jumped up at her.

"Oh, you naughty boy!" said Mrs Smik. "Did you fly our shuttle, all by yourself?"

Dog-dog said nothing, but as he turned to go, I'm sure he winked at me. I am almost certain he will be back some day, to eat more fungus pie.

Answers and mark scheme

Set A English reading

Paper 1: reading prompt and answer booklet

The Story of Grace Darling

a a lighthouse keeper's daughter

b Longstone Lighthouse

1 He kept the light burning in the lighthouse. **(1 mark)**

2 lonely ☐ important ☐
dangerous ☑ burning ☐ **(1 mark)**

3 7 ☐ 63 ☑
18 ☐ 38 ☐ **(1 mark)**

4 Any two from: the engine stopped; the crew could not use the sails; because of the storm.
(1 mark: two correct for 1 mark)

5 Grace/She told her father about it. **(1 mark)**

6 Any answers that refer to people clinging to the rocks/people still alive. **(1 mark)**

7 stormy **(1 mark)**

8

2	1
3	4

(1 mark: award 1 mark for the pictures correctly numbered)

9 People wrote songs about Grace. ☐
People thought Grace was very brave. ☑
Grace's picture was on postcards. ☐
Queen Victoria heard Grace's story. ☐
(1 mark)

Why Owls have Big Eyes

c get together ☐
at home ☐
early in the morning ☑
in the woods ☐

d more owls than pigeons

10 Any one from: (because) the Big Wood/it had lots of trees; (because) they needed a big place. **(1 mark)**

11 in two weeks ☐ today ☐
later this week ☐ in one week ☑ **(1 mark)**

12 Because the trees were full. **(1 mark)**

13 certain ☑ safe ☐
trust ☐ truthful ☐ **(1 mark)**

14 pigeon wings **(1 mark)**

15 To laugh at the pigeons. ☐
To make room for the pigeons. ☑
To watch the pigeons. ☐
To welcome the pigeons. ☐ **(1 mark)**

16 It was getting late. ☐ They felt cold. ☐
They felt nervous. ☑ There was no room for them. ☑
(1 mark: award 1 mark for two correct answers ticked)

17 The owls flew off. ☐4 The owls became worried. ☐3
More pigeons arrived. ☐1 The owls were surprised. ☐2
(1 mark: award 1 mark for correct order)

18 Any of the following answers are acceptable.

Yes, because:

- the owls were surprised to see so many pigeons.
- the owls felt nervous because there were so many pigeons.
- the owls flew away because there were more pigeons than owls.
- there were so many pigeons that they were like a huge grey cloud. **(1 mark)**

19 They/Owls fly at night; They/Owls stare; They/Owls look out for pigeons.
(1 mark: two correct for 1 mark)

20 Any plausible, text-based answers are acceptable, e.g. They felt (very) happy/delighted/overjoyed, because:

- the owls had flown off/left.
- they had won the contest.
- there were more pigeons than owls.
- they had shown/proved there are more pigeons than owls. **(1 mark)**

Set A English reading

Paper 2: reading booklet

Why Spiders have Thin Legs

1 Any justified reason, derived from the text, e.g.
   - Anansi was greedy.
   - Anansi loved food/delicious food. **(1 mark)**

2 black and hairy ☐
   short and thick ☑
   long and thin ☐
   tired and weak ☐ **(1 mark)**

3 Any one of the following:
   - he was very busy/lazy
   - he didn't want to do any jobs/work/sweep the floor/
     wash the dishes. **(1 mark)**

4 beans and rice (Accept a delicious meal) **(1 mark)**

5 So Monkey could tug when the banana bread
   was ready. **(1 mark)**

6 a)
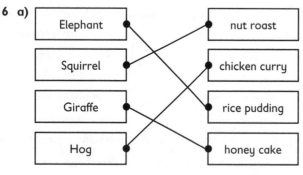

Elephant	nut roast
Squirrel	chicken curry
Giraffe	rice pudding
Hog	honey cake

   (1 mark)

   b) To tug on the web **(1 mark)**

7 His mouth watered. (Accept Anansi's mouth watered.)
   (1 mark)

8 The river washed the webs away. ☐4
   Rabbit tugged a web. ☐2
   Anansi talked to Fox. ☐1
   Anansi's legs started to grow long and skinny. ☐3

   (1 mark: award 1 mark for correct order)

Water

9 washing our clothes. ☑
   burning wood. ☐
   plants to grow. ☑
   drying our clothes. ☐

(1 mark: award 1 mark for two correct answers ticked)

10 droplets **(1 mark)**

11 a circle of events that happen again and again in the
   same order. **(1 mark)**

12

| water falls as rain, hail, snow or sleet | | water changes from liquid into gas |

(1 mark: award 1 mark for both correct labels)

13 Any one of the following: water droplets move into the
   air; water changes from a liquid into a gas. **(1 mark)**

14 blood 80%; skin 70%
   (1 mark: both correct for 1 mark)

15 Any three of the following: storms; floods; animal
   waste; food waste; chemicals such as oil; refuse
   (1 mark: three correct answers for 1 mark)

16 Any two of the following: waste; refuse; litter
   (1 mark: two correct answers for 1 mark)

17 Any one of the following: only 1% of the world's water
   is fresh and safe to drink; most of the world's water is
   salty and we can't drink it; we need water every day.

   (1 mark)

18

The information says that...	True	False
humans cause all polluted water.		✓
we should try to save water.	✓	
90% of the world's water is not fresh.		✓
you should pick up your litter, but only when you are at a beach, lake or river.		✓
a watering can uses less water than a hosepipe.	✓	

**(2 marks for four correct answers, 1 mark for
two or three correct answers)**

Set A English grammar, punctuation and spelling

Paper 1: spelling

These are the correct spellings:

1 skate
2 claws
3 trunk
4 nearest
5 feather
6 telephone
7 match
8 pushes
9 Wednesday
10 sandcastle
11 nothing
12 brother
13 wrist
14 purple
15 quarrel
16 chalk
17 bony
18 useful
19 festival
20 invitation

(20 marks: 1 mark for each correct spelling)

Set A English grammar, punctuation and spelling

Paper 2: questions

a Any suitable present tense verb ending in -ing, e.g. reading, holding, carrying, buying.

b full stop ☐
question mark ✓
exclamation mark ☐
comma ☐

1 (it) is a hot day. (sally) and (tom) are eating ice cream.

(1 mark: all three correctly circled for 1 mark)

2 and ☐   or ✓
but ☐   so ☐   **(1 mark)**

3 on holiday this year! ☐
on holiday this year. ☐
on holiday this year ☐
on holiday this year? ✓   **(1 mark)**

4

Sentence	Full stop	Question mark
You can have tea at our house	✓	
Are you coming to play football		✓
Where are my shoes		✓
It is lunchtime now	✓	

(1 mark: all correct for 1 mark)

5 a verb ☐   a noun ✓
an adjective ☐   an adverb ☐   **(1 mark)**

6 What a wonderful surprise it was!   **(1 mark)**

7 questions ☐   commands ☐
exclamations ☐   statements ✓   **(1 mark)**

8 Green (plants) need (air), (water) and (sunlight) to grow.

(1 mark: all four correct for 1 mark)

9 happy ☐   inhappy ☐
unhappy ✓   imhappy ☐   **(1 mark)**

10 In the garden, a <u>cheeky</u> robin hopped onto a branch and he sang a <u>sweet</u> song.

(1 mark: both adjectives underlined for 1 mark)

11 Did you see that colour**ful** rainbow in the sky?
The fear**less** explorer went bravely into the jungle.

(1 mark: two correct suffixes added for 1 mark)

12 an adverb ✓   a noun ☐
an adjective ☐   a verb ☐   **(1 mark)**

13 You must bring a coat, gloves, a hat, boots and a packed lunch to school on Friday.

(1 mark: three correctly placed commas for 1 mark)

14 ran (Accept was running, has run or had run)   **(1 mark)**

15 Any response that explains that the apostrophe shows belonging or possession, e.g.

- it shows belonging/possession
- it shows that a/the desk belongs to a/the teacher
- because a/the desk belongs to a/the teacher.

Responses that meet the criteria but use different phrasing should also be marked as correct.

Do not accept responses referring to other uses of the apostrophe, e.g.

- because a letter/letters have been missed out
- because it is short for is/it is.   **(1 mark)**

16 were   **(1 mark)**

17 Award 2 marks for any command sentence that starts with a capital letter and ends with an appropriate punctuation mark, e.g.

- No, don't do that, Brandon!
- That's a bad idea!
- Stop it, Brandon.

Award 1 mark for any command sentence that does not start with a capital letter and/or that does not end with a full stop or an exclamation mark, e.g.

- no don't do that brandon
- you must not do that

Responses that meet the criteria but use different phrasing should be marked as correct.

Correct spelling is not required for the award of the mark. Although correct sentence punctuation is required for the award of both marks, pupils are not required to use capital letters correctly for Brandon or correct internal punctuation. **(2 marks)**

18 used (Accept was using, had used or has used)
chose (Accept had chosen or have chosen)
(2 marks: 1 mark for each correct answer)

Set B English reading

Paper 1: reading prompt and answer booklet

a in the south-east of Europe

b Any two from: a mainland; mountains; small islands.

1

The Severn	☐
The United Kingdom	☑
England	☐
The River Severn	☐

(1 mark)

2 England **(1 mark)**

3

Greece has more people than Wales.	☑
Wales has more islands than Greece.	☐
Greece's capital city is Athens.	☑
Mount Olympus is the highest mountain in Wales.	☐

(1 mark: award 1 mark for two correct answers ticked)

4 Any reference to usually hot weather in summer, e.g.

- the weather is usually very hot in the summer
- because it's usually hot in summer. **(1 mark)**

5

flag	☐	population	☑
capital	☐	million	☐

(1 mark)

Special Shoes

c in a small village

d

	Lena liked	Maya liked
rounders		✓
hopscotch		✓
reading	✓	
drawing	✓	
dancing		✓

6

because Lena was lazy	☐
because Lena was tired	☐
because Lena thought Maya was lazy	☑
because Lena thought Maya was tired	☐

(1 mark)

7 Any **two** of the following:

- (because) she could pick enough (by herself)
- (because her) Mum would be pleased
- (so that) they could all eat them with cream for tea.

(1 mark)

8 nowhere **(1 mark)**

9 "It's your lucky day!" ☐

"Aha!" ☐

"That's for me to know, and for you to find out." ☐

"Hello Lena." ☑

(1 mark)

10 curious ☑ frightened ☐

annoyed ☐ hungry ☐ **(1 mark)**

11 special shoes **(1 mark)**

12 She gasped. **(1 mark)**

13 Any answer that quotes or paraphrases the following:

the soles were clean and shiny, e.g.

- the soles were new

- the soles were not worn. **(1 mark)**

14 She/the old lady vanished. (Accept she/the old lady disappeared) **(1 mark)**

15 warm ☐ very cold ☑

hot ☐ very hot ☐ **(1 mark)**

16 tired ☐ surprised ☑

bored ☐ upset ☐ **(1 mark)**

17 Any one of the following:

- she poked Maya/her

- she called, "Time to go home!"

- she told her it was time to go home

- she said, "Wakey-wakey, Lazybones!"

- she called her Lazybones and told her to wake up.

(1 mark)

18 Any answer that quotes or paraphrases the following:

- because Maya/she blinked

- because Maya's/her mouth fell open.

(1 mark)

19 What/other things they/the shoes could do **(1 mark)**

20 Lena put the shoes on. ☐4

Lena met an old lady. ☐2

Lena's sister fell asleep. ☐1

Lena traded the raspberries for a shoe box. ☐3

(1 mark: award 1 mark for correct order)

Set B English reading

Paper 2: reading booklet

All about Bees

1 three (Accept 3) **(1 mark)**

2 always female ☑

live for up to one year ☐

mate with the queen bee ☐

die after stinging ☑

(1 mark: award 1 mark for two correct answers ticked)

3 To show the other bees where the food is. (Accept to show other bees where there are flowers with a lot of nectar and pollen) **(1 mark)**

4 Any two of the following: use of chemicals; loss of habitat; lack of food; poisons in the air **(1 mark)**

5 Any two of the following: plants would not be pollinated; some plants would not grow new seeds; some/flower/fruit/nut/vegetable plants would die **(1 mark)**

6 essential **(1 mark)**

7 Pollen helps other flowers to make seeds. ☐4

The bee moves to other flowers. ☐2

The pollen rubs off the bee's body. ☐3

Pollen from a flower sticks to the bee's body. ☐1

(1 mark: award 1 mark for correct order)

8

Words		Meanings
protect		making flowers
habitats		natural homes
flowering		keep safe

(protect → keep safe; habitats → natural homes; flowering → making flowers)

(1 mark)

Alien on Board

9 Any one of the following: their/a teacher; a computer; not really a person (Do not accept very lifelike, strict) **(1 mark)**

10 Any one of the following: it was very quiet; it was very dark; it was very dark, except for the stars; they had never seen any aliens/monsters/creatures. **(1 mark)**

11 They heard a buzz and a loud crash. (Accept they heard a loud noise/loud noises) **(1 mark)**

12 the most furry ☐

the most odd ☑

the most strong ☐

the most friendly ☐ **(1 mark)**

13 Zoe/she did not like it. (Accept Zoe/she was frightened of it. Do not accept Zoe/she wanted it to go away.) **(1 mark)**

14 terrified **(1 mark)**

15 Any two of the following: she went up to it; she knelt down; she spoke to it gently; she told it not to be afraid/ she said, "Don't be afraid"; she said "We won't hurt you!"

(1 mark: two correct answers for 1 mark)

16 Any reference to the alien belonging to Mr and Mrs Smik, e.g.

• it/the alien belonged to Mr and Mrs Smik

• it/the alien was the property of Mr and Mrs Smik

• its/the alien's owners were Mr and Mrs Smik.

Also accept:

• they need to take it/the alien home to its owners

• it/the alien does not belong to Skylar. **(1 mark)**

17 a)

The story says that Mr and Mrs Smik...	True	False
have five long sticks.		✓
have tentacles.		✓
have very little fur.	✓	
have pale pink skin.	✓	
have lumpy skin.		✓

(2 marks: two or three correct for 1 mark, four correct for 2 marks)

b) Any reference to human beings, e.g.

• they were human beings

• they were humans

• they looked like humans

• they were probably human beings. **(1 mark)**

18 Any reference to dog-dog winking at Skylar, e.g.

• because she is sure dog-dog winked at her

• because she thinks dog-dog winked at her

• because she thinks dog-dog will be back to eat more fungus pie. **(1 mark)**

Set B English grammar, punctuation and spelling

Paper 1: spelling

These are the correct spellings:

1 skill

2 parcel

3 hatch

4 puppy

5 circus

6 clear

7 watches

8 chopping

9 Thursday

10 shy

11 easier

12 health

13 above

14 cabbage

15 hurries

16 wasn't

17 nephew

18 valley

19 ladybird

20 action

(20 marks: 1 mark for each correct spelling)

Set B English grammar, punctuation and spelling

Paper 2: questions

a smallest ☐   small ☐

most small ☐   smaller ☑

b don't

1 Do you like my new green hat?

(1 mark: all words correctly underlined for 1 mark)

2 My birthday is in april and jane's birthday is in may.

(1 mark: three capital letters identified for 1 mark)

3 full stop ☐

exclamation mark ☐

question mark ☑

comma ☐ **(1 mark)**

4 Our school trip is to Leeds Castle. **(1 mark)**

5 a noun ☐   an adjective ☐

an adverb ☐   a verb ☑ **(1 mark)**

6 What a great idea I have ☐
What a great idea I have! ☑
What a great idea I have? ☐
What a great idea I have, ☐ **(1 mark)**

7 We all cheered (loudly) when my sister won the race. **(1 mark)**

8 stayed ☑ stays ☐
staying ☐ to stay ☐ **(1 mark)**

9

	Present tense	Past tense
I was talking to Mary.		✓
Jack is brushing his teeth.	✓	

(1 mark: both ticked correctly for 1 mark)

10 statements ☐ exclamations ☑
commands ☐ questions ☐ **(1 mark)**

11 How exciting! We're going on holiday! ☐
Have you got the tickets? ☐
Carry your suitcase to the car. ☐
I have locked the front door. ☑ **(1 mark)**

12 Spring, summer, autumn and winter are the four seasons of the year.
(1 mark: both commas correctly placed for 1 mark)

13 We are going to the shop and buying some ice cream. ☐
We went to the shop and bought some ice cream. ☑
We go to the shop and bought some ice cream. ☐
We went to the shop and buy some ice cream. ☐ **(1 mark)**

14 When we woke up in the morning, the (soft) (white) snow was falling silently from the sky.
(1 mark: both adjectives circled for 1 mark)

15 He can't go swimming today.
I hope he'll be better tomorrow.
(2 marks: 1 mark for each correct sentence)

16 They is closing the paddling pool. ☐
The park is closing soon. ☑
Peter is closing the door quietly. ☑
I are closing my eyes and counting to ten. ☐
(1 mark: two ticked correctly for 1 mark)

17

When we got home it was time for bed.		question
Pass the salt.		exclamation
When is it lunchtime?		statement
How much I love it!		command

(1 mark)

18 Award 2 marks for an appropriate, grammatically correct sentence, with correct use of capital letters and end punctuation, e.g.
- It is a birthday party.
- They are wearing party hats.

Award 1 mark for an appropriate, grammatically correct sentence, with incorrect use of capital letters and / or end punctuation, e.g.
- today is his birthday.
- he blows the candles out

Do not accept a phrase (with or without correct punctuation), e.g.
- a birthday party
- lots of balloons

(2 marks)

Spelling test administration

Ensure that your child has a pen or pencil and a rubber to complete the paper.

Your child is not allowed to use a dictionary or electronic spell checker.

Ask your child to look at the practice spelling question. Do this question together.

For each question, read out the word that your child will need to spell correctly.

Then read the whole sentence.

Then read the word again.

Your child needs to write the word into the blank space in the sentence.

Here is the practice question for Set A:

The word is **play**.

The children **play** in the park.

The word is **play**.

Check that your child understands that 'play' should be written in the first blank space.

Explain that you are going to read 20 sentences. Each sentence has a word missing, just like the practice question.

Read questions 1 to 20 to your child, starting with the question number, reading out the word followed by the sentence, and then the word again.

Leave enough time (at least 12 seconds) between questions for your child to attempt the spelling. Do not rush, as the test time of 15 minutes is approximate and children will be given more time if they need it.

Tell your child that they may cross out the word and write it again if they think they have made a mistake.

You may repeat the target word if needed.

Set A English grammar, punctuation and spelling

Paper 1: spelling

Practice question: The word is **play**.
The children **play** in the park.
The word is **play**.

Spelling 1: The word is **skate**.
The ice is too thin to **skate** on.
The word is **skate**.

Spelling 2: The word is **claws**.
Our cat has long **claws**.
The word is **claws**.

Spelling 3: The word is **trunk**.
An elephant's nose is called a **trunk**.
The word is **trunk**.

Spelling 4: The word is **nearest**.
Sit in the chair **nearest** the door.
The word is **nearest**.

Spelling 5: The word is **feather**.
Sally found a magpie **feather**.
The word is **feather**.

Spelling 6: The word is **telephone**.
Please give me your **telephone** number.
The word is **telephone**.

Spelling 7: The word is **match**.
We all enjoyed the cricket **match**.
The word is **match**.

Spelling 8: The word is **pushes**.
Dad **pushes** Milly's pram.
The word is **pushes**.

Spelling 9: The word is **Wednesday**.
We are going swimming on
Wednesday.
The word is **Wednesday**.

Spelling 10: The word is **sandcastle**.
We build a **sandcastle** on the beach.
The word is **sandcastle**.

Spelling 11: The word is **nothing**.
Hannah has **nothing** to do today.
The word is **nothing**.

Spelling 12: The word is **brother**.
My **brother** loves playing football.
The word is **brother**.

Spelling 13: The word is **wrist**.
You wear a watch on your **wrist**.
The word is **wrist**.

Spelling 14: The word is **purple**.
The hat is **purple** with yellow flowers.
The word is **purple**.

Spelling 15: The word is **quarrel**.
I do not want to **quarrel** with you.
The word is **quarrel**.

Spelling 16: The word is **chalk**.
Please pass me the pink **chalk**.
The word is **chalk**.

Spelling 17: The word is **bony**.
This fish is very **bony**.
The word is **bony**.

Spelling 18: The word is **useful**.
Plastic is a **useful** material.
The word is **useful**.

Spelling 19: The word is **festival**.
Our school has a **festival** in
September.
The word is **festival**.

Spelling 20: The word is **invitation**.
Alex gave me an **invitation** to his
party.
The word is **invitation**.

Set B English grammar, punctuation and spelling

Paper 1: spelling

Practice question: The word is **flew**.
The birds **flew** into the sky.
The word is **flew**.

Spelling 1: The word is **skill**.
Gina shows great **skill** on the piano.
The word is **skill**.

Spelling 2: The word is **parcel**.
The postman brought a big **parcel**.
The word is **parcel**.

Spelling 3: The word is **hatch**.
The eggs **hatch** under the hen.
The word is **hatch**.

Spelling 4: The word is **puppy**.
Our new **puppy** loves to play
with us.
The word is **puppy**.

Spelling 5: The word is **circus**.
The children had an amazing time
at the **circus**.
The word is **circus**.

Spelling 6: The word is **clear**.
The sky was **clear** when we left
home.
The word is **clear**.

Spelling 7: The word is **watches**.
Tom **watches** TV after he has done
his homework.
The word is **watches**.

Spelling 8: The word is **chopping**.
Dad is **chopping** vegetables for
dinner.
The word is **chopping**.

Spelling 9: The word is **Thursday**.
Gran is coming to tea on **Thursday**.
The word is **Thursday**.

Spelling 10: The word is **shy**.
Jane was too **shy** to join in our
game.
The word is **shy**.

Spelling 11: The word is **easier**.
He thinks reading is **easier** than
writing.
The word is **easier**.

Spelling 12: The word is **health**.
Eating fresh fruit every day is good
for your **health**.
The word is **health**.

Spelling 13: The word is **above**.
The hot air balloon rose **above**
the rooftops.
The word is **above**.

Spelling 14: The word is **cabbage**.
She loves all vegetables, especially
cabbage.
The word is **cabbage**.

Spelling 15: The word is **hurries**.
Mum **hurries** to answer the door.
The word is **hurries**.

Spelling 16: The word is **wasn't**.
Jane **wasn't** at school today.
The word is **wasn't**.

Spelling 17: The word is **nephew**.
Uncle Toby took his **nephew** to
the park.
The word is **nephew**.

Spelling 18: The word is **valley**.
The river runs through a deep **valley**.
The word is **valley**.

Spelling 19: The word is **ladybird**.
Yesterday I saw a **ladybird** with seven
spots.
The word is **ladybird**.

Spelling 20: The word is **action**.
I enjoy reading stories with lots of
action.
The word is **action**.